Attract, Capture & Convert:

89 Simple Ways Entrepreneurs Make Money Online (& Offline) Using Social Media & Web Marketing Strategy

Mason Duchatschek
Adam Burns
Adam Kreitman

Copyright 2014 - All Rights Reserved

No part of this publication may be reproduced or transmitted in any form or by any means, mechanical or electronic, including photocopying and recording, or by any information storage and retrieval system, without permission in writing from the authors or publisher (except by a reviewer, who may quote brief passages and/or show brief video clips in a review).

Disclaimer: The Publisher and the Authors make no representations or warranties in any form or by any means with respect to the accuracy or completeness of the contents of this work and specifically disclaim all warranties, including (without limitation) warranties of fitness for a particular purpose. No warranty may be created or extended by sales or promotional materials. The advice and strategies contained herein may not be suitable for every situation, person, nonprofit organization, or business. This work is sold with the understanding that the Publisher is not engaged in rendering legal, accounting, or other related professional services. If professional assistance is required, the services of a competent professional person should be sought. Neither the Publisher nor the Authors shall be liable for damages arising herefrom. The fact that an organization or website is referred to in this work as a citation and/or a potential source of further information does not mean that the Author or the Publisher endorses the information the organization or website may provide or recommendations it may make. In some, but not all, cases, affiliate income may be generated to the authors from products or services purchased by readers from sites that are referred to in this work. Further, readers should be aware that Internet websites listed in this work may have changed or disappeared between when this work was written and when it is read.

Table of Contents

Section 1: The Big Picture Overview: The Strategy Behind What Needs to Be Accomplished, Why, and How! 17

    The Credibility Ladder 17

    Becoming Your Own Media Outlet 20

    Building Your Audience: Old Vs. New 22

    Sales Vs. Marketing 23

    The Next Endangered Species: Salespeople? 25

    What DO People Trust? 26

    Sales = Closing Percentage × Number of Selling Opportunities . 28

    Virtual Marketing, Sales & Customer Service 31

    How to Win Before You Begin 32

    Jug Fishing = Internet Marketing 34

    Automate & Dominate 36

    Twitter: Introductions, Curiosity & the Law of Attraction 38

    YouTube: Introductions, Curiosity & the Law of Attraction 40

    Sorting Vs. Convincing: Work With the Willing 41

    The Online Land Rush: Act Now 43

Section 2: 89 of the Best Ways to Attract, Capture & Convert Prospects Online (& Offline) 47

    Mistake 1: Failing to Love the Haters 47

    Mistake 2: Cold-Calling Prospects Who Should Be Calling You 48

    Mistake 3: Failure to Let the Message and/or Product Be the Star When Using Web Videos 49

Mistake 4: Failure to Eliminate Resistance Before It Occurs 49

Mistake 5: Showcasing Bad Grammar, Punctuation, and Spelling (or Not Putting Out Content Because of It) 50

Mistake 6: Failure to Point Out Benefits 50

Mistake 7: Leaders Driving Slow in the Fast Lane 51

Mistake 8: Failing to Begin With the Ideal Outcome in Mind 52

Mistake 9: Ignoring the Warning Signs...53

Mistake 10: Lack of Focus on Genuine, Unique, and Authentic Content..54

Mistake 11: Putting the Cart Before the Horse..............................55

Mistake 12: Being Sterile, Politically Correct, and Forgettable...56

Mistake 13: Bragging 57

Mistake 14: Failure to Make Your Fans Part of Your Creative Process and Product/Service Development 57

Mistake 15: Snubbing Your Fan Club 58

Mistake 16: Only Knocking Down One Pin (Failing to Put Out Content in Multiple Places in Multiple Formats) 59

Mistake 17: Failure to Capture Leads and Follow Up..................60

Mistake 18: Failing to Sell What's Free 61

Mistake 19: Failing to Educate, Entertain, or Inspire 62

Mistake 20: Location, Location, Location....................................63

Mistake 21: Emotional Attachments 63

Mistake 22: Failing to Think (and Act) Like a Rock Star 64

Mistake 23: Creating Commercials 65

Mistake 24: Becoming a One Trick Pony 66

Mistake 25: Failing to Answer Objections and Frequently Asked Questions 67
Mistake 26: Confusing Rank With Authority and Trying to Lead Anyway..68
Mistake 27: Trying to Understand Everything Before Doing Anything 70
Mistake 28: Failure to Realize That Text Is Good; Pictures Are Better; Videos Are the Best 70
Mistake 29: Blending In 70
Mistake 30: Resistance to Change...71
Mistake 31: Running From Problems..72
Mistake 32: Trying to Hide Mistakes 72
Mistake 33: No Special Offer 73
Mistake 34: No Free Samples and/or Interaction 74
Mistake 35: Letting a Hot Lead Get Cold 75
Mistake 36: Failure to Appeal to Those Who Want to Work and Play 76
Mistake 37: Worrying About What Others Are Doing 77
Mistake 38: Bringing the Boredom 77
Mistake 39: Chasing the "Next Big Thing".....................................78
Mistake 40: Failing to Focus on the Fundamentals 79
Mistake 41: Failing to Give People What They Want ... First 79
Mistake 42: Writing Scripts for Search Engines Instead of People 81
Mistake 43: Forfeit and Non-participation 81

Mistake 44: Failing to Market Globally Even If Your Prospects Are Local 82

Mistake 45: Failure to Reap the Rewards of Failed Ad Campaigns 83

Mistake 46: Ignoring Your Ratings 83

Mistake 47: Failure to Make Heroes Out of Influencers 84

Mistake 48: Failure to Recognize the Market Value of Your Online Real Estate 85

Mistake 49: Forgetting the Relationship Between Offline Service and Online Sales 86

Mistake 50: Creating Content That Won't Get Discovered or Engage Ideal Prospects 88

Mistake 51: Failure to Position as a Better Alternative 88

Mistake 52: Failing to Create Content That Features Your Competition 89

Mistake 53: Failing to Work With the Willing 90

Mistake 54: Failure to Create Evangelists 90

Mistake 55: Playing It Too Safe 92

Mistake 56: Unnecessarily Using Pushy Salespeople 93

Mistake 57: Failure to Diversify Your Online Lead Sources 93

Mistake 58: Trying to Catch Fish in Empty Ponds 94

Mistake 59: Not Marketing to the Maybes 94

Mistake 60: Being Too Slick /Lacking Authenticity 94

Mistake 61: Forgetting That a Little Customer Can Have a Big Voice 95

Mistake 62: Giving Up Too Soon 96

Mistake 63: Advertising for Your Competitors 98

Mistake 64: Doing What Everyone Else Is Doing 98

Mistake 65: Relying on Just One Source of Traffic 100

Mistake 66: Caring More About Your Sales Process than a Customer's Buying Process 101

Mistake 67: Failing to Offer Your Products or Services for Sale Online Using eCommerce 101

Mistake 68: Letting Egos and Attitudes Kill Sales......................102

Mistake 69: Making Customers Jump Through Too Many Hoops 102

Mistake 70: Not Doing the Research...103

Mistake 71: Failure to Minimize Client Exposure to Human Error and Misunderstanding..104

Mistake 72: Paying Unnecessary Commissions........................104

Mistake 73: Spending Time With Employee Drama Instead of Customers 104

Mistake 74: Monitoring Fiction Over Fact..................................105

Mistake 75: Losing Top Talent Unnecessarily............................105

Mistake 76: Paying Too Much for Sales Training 106

Mistake 77: Lack of Knowledge When It's Needed Most 106

Mistake 78: Sending Employees Mixed Messages 107

Mistake 79: Allowing Institutional Knowledge to Escape 107

Mistake 80: Relying Too Heavily on Your Reps and Their Customer Relationships..108

Mistake 81: Assuming Your Ideal Prospects Like What YOU Like 108

Mistake 82: Failing to Connect the Dots for Prospects and Customers 109

Mistake 83: Inflexible/Inaccessible Content Management Systems and Websites 109

Mistake 84: Forgetting There's No F***ing Erase Button on the Internet 110

Mistake 85: Creating Sites/Content That Is Not Mobile-Friendly 110

Mistake 86: Failure to Recognize and Build Your Goldmine (Your Prospect and Customer Lists) 111

Mistake 87: Being Afraid to Invest in Paid Online Advertising 111

Mistake 88: Being Busy Instead of Productive 113

Mistake 89: Focusing on Traffic, Not Conversions 115

SECTION 3: The Bonuses (Did we save the best for last? You be the judge.) 119

Super Bonus Strategy #1: - DEFENDING YOUR GOOD NAME 119

Super Bonus Strategy #2 - Using YOUR COMPETITORS' Advertising Budget Against Them (This one is a doozy!) 121

Super Bonus Strategy #3 - Unleashing Our Top Four Secret Weapons 124

(For Video and Online Marketing) 124

Secret Weapon #1 - Want to know where to send your content and AUTOMATE your content distribution? 125

Secret Weapon #2 - Want to introduce your YouTube channel and videos to HUNDREDS of TARGETED and ACTIVE users

EACH DAY who are MUCH more likely to SPREAD THE
WORD about you and your expertise?..128
Secret Weapon #3 - Our favorite keyword research tool: Get
found on search engines. 128
Secret Weapon #4 - Get Professional Videos Produced for 90-
95% Less Than Other High-End (High-Definition) Studios......129
Super Bonus GIVEAWAY #4 - We have a BIG SURPRISE for
YOU! 129

About the Authors:..131
    Mason Duchatschek..131
    Adam Burns..131
    Adam Kreitman 132

Welcome:

If you don't ever want to spend another soul-crushing day working for the man then pay close attention.

If you want your freedom, but aren't that tech-savvy, it's OK. You don't have to be.

We realize you went into business, or are looking to go into business, to do what you do best and like to do most.

Maybe you're struggling with ideas on how to start a business or work from home.

Maybe your current new business development strategies for your existing small business or home business aren't working like they used to.

Maybe your budget is small or nonexistent and you have to be incredibly lean and resourceful to get the most out of every dollar you invest in your business, and your margins for error are slim.

If any of the above apply to you, then you're in for some pleasant surprises.

We're going to highlight and discuss a number of online and offline marketing mistakes that entrepreneurs make every day that you should avoid at all costs. We'll showcase mistakes they don't want to publicly admit or let anyone else know they made.

It's expensive and embarrassing to learn these lessons the hard way. You DON'T want to experience them on your own dime.

We built this book to be a quick read, but the information contained in it is extremely powerful. It gives you an insider's look that is easy to understand and full of real-world examples that are practical, helpful, and inspiring.

What's in it for you? You should walk away with valuable insights and key ideas that can help you attract, capture, and convert more of your ideal prospects into customers right away. You can do it online and offline, even if you're not a "techie."

We will point out all kinds of common and unnecessary mistakes OTHER people make every day (so you don't repeat them). All you need to do is avoid them and/or do the opposite and you will have the best ways to make money online (and offline) using social media and web marketing strategy.

Of course, you'll have to know your products, your services, and the benefits associated with them. But, what good business owner doesn't?

In summary, you will discover:

1) What business trends are emerging and why (so you make the right moves instead of the wrong ones).
2) The importance of good keyword research (and the best tools to help you do it right the first time, quickly and easily).
3) The importance of creating useful content that serves your ideal prospects as well as other people who take care of them too (so you can get OTHER people promoting YOU effortlessly).
4) The importance of creating your content in all kinds of different formats (blogs, articles, videos, podcasts, social media posts, etc.) so your prospects find YOU when they're ready to buy.
5) The power of video and YouTube marketing (so you can sell your products, solve customer problems, and train employees online without having to add or manage unnecessary additional headcount).
6) The most common online and offline marketing mistakes and how to avoid them.

There are all kinds of new business books and "how to" books that talk about web marketing strategy, social media marketing, and ways to make money online.

Unfortunately, most of them require you to try and become an expert at Facebook marketing, YouTube marketing (video marketing), Twitter marketing, Pinterest marketing, LinkedIn marketing, blogging, website design, and more. We doubt you have that much spare time to be playing around on the Internet when you've got a business to run.

The thing is, you don't have to be an expert in any of those things. (In fact, you're better off not focusing on just one form of marketing.)

And even if you're not an expert in those things, you can still learn how to ...

... sell online 24 hours a day, 365 days a year, worldwide to an almost unlimited number of ideal prospects (even if you don't have, or ever want to hire, train, manage, or PAY salespeople). That's right. Keep the money in your pocket that you OTHERWISE would have paid to salespeople.

... attract more of your IDEAL prospects so you and/or your staff don't get bogged down with overly needy, impossible-to-please whiners you wish you never had to deal with. You know the type.

... use strategies to get found online when people are looking to buy what you have to sell regardless of which social media sites become more popular or fade away.

We'll also identify and tell you how to access links to some of our favorite online tools and "secret weapons" that we use to AUTOMATE time-consuming (but VERY necessary) tasks. Until recently, we only shared these "secret weapons" with our private consulting clients.

The fact that you're here, right now, gives you an unfair advantage if you're willing to use it. We want you to take the right actions in the right places at the right times so your business grows and you can have more fun and freedom as it does.

We also don't want you to learn painful and expensive lessons that could unnecessarily ruin your relationships with your friends and family, cost you your business, or force you to update your résumé in the hopes of landing a soul-crushing job working for the man.

Knowing what to do to grow your business isn't enough. Avoiding mistakes that can ruin your best opportunities isn't either.

You have to take action. And you have to find ways to relentlessly make forward progress and KEEP taking action even when obstacles appear before you and unwelcome burdens try to slow you down.

So here's the deal. We want to help you recognize opportunities you might have missed. We want you to avoid mistakes you might have otherwise made. Most importantly, we want you to do what needs to be done, and that might take some convincing. We get it.

We're not asking you to trust us. We will spell it out for you. We will explain why it is important to take a particular action or avoid another. We will keep explaining why and continue to add to the reasons because that's what it's going to take to get some of you, perhaps most of you, to APPLY what you're about to read.

We didn't write this so you could read it. We wrote it so you could DO it.

We help entrepreneurs and the marketing people who work for them attract, capture, and convert more of their ideal prospects into customers online, even if they aren't techies and don't like or understand social media marketing.

We wrote this book for multiple reasons.

The politically correct thing to say is we wrote this because we're thankful for all the people in our lives who opened up windows of opportunity around us, encouraged us, and shared their wisdom when we asked for it. And that's true. We are thankful to all of those people (and there are a lot of them). And we do feel a great sense of personal responsibility to share the gifts of knowledge and experience that have been given to us over the years.

But it's more than that.

We see people every day doing the best they can with what they have. It's not enough. Some know it. Others haven't realized it.

They're losing their sleep, their health, their hope, their families, their businesses, their sense of self-worth, and their BEST opportunities. Some don't know which way is up. It sucks. It's hard. It hurts and we want to help. So we're going to.

We want to see if we could actually get people to DO something powerful with these ideas. We want you to avoid unnecessary disasters. We want you to seize opportunities you know are yours!

Some people only need one or two good reasons to do something before they take action. Others need a bunch. The rest choose to learn the hard way (trial and error), even though they don't have to.

We are all insanely passionate about this stuff. We see, every day, the huge impact it can have on businesses and, more importantly, the people in those businesses.

But this stuff is overwhelming and there's so much garbage and snake oil being peddled out there that lead people down rabbit holes crawling with, well, snakes. We want to help you avoid those rabbit holes.

We wrote this book to help guide you down a proven path to independence, success, wealth, and happiness. And we want you to have some fun, too.

Section 1: The Big Picture Overview: The Strategy Behind What Needs to Be Accomplished, Why, and How!

Here's the deal. We plan to lay out a vision of what needs to be accomplished and why it is important. Then we will reveal the top ways even "low-tech" entrepreneurs make money, both online and offline, using social media and web marketing strategies.

Lastly, we'll expose and discuss many of the biggest mistakes of business owners and marketers that make them crash and burn on the road to success.

Don't make those mistakes and you'll have the top ways to make money online and offline using social media and the web staring you in the face.

It's that simple.

Oh, and by the way, we promised you "89 Ways" in the title of this book, but in the spirit of delivering more than we promise, we're throwing in some bonus ideas, too!

Let's get to it.

The Credibility Ladder

Want to increase the demand for what you and your company offer?

Want to get paid more for it?

It's easy: Reduce the risk. Here's how.

The demand for what you offer and the price people are willing to pay for it are greatly affected by your ideal prospects' perceived risk. Your ideal prospects don't want to make a mistake. They don't want to have to apologize or defend their decision to do business with you, and they certainly don't want to waste more time and money fixing unnecessary problems that could have been avoided in the first place.

The lower you, your company, or your product ranks on what my friend Brett Curry, a marketing consultant out of Springfield, Missouri (see http://www.OnlineMarketingGiant.com), and I like to refer to as the "Credibility Ladder"... the more perceived risk is associated with doing business with you.

The higher you are on the Credibility Ladder, the greater the demand there is for you, your company, or your offering, generally resulting in people willing to pay more.

The objective of your marketing efforts should be to climb that Credibility Ladder as fast as possible and stay up there.

What separates those at the top of the ladder from those at the bottom? How did they get there? How do you get there? How long does it take? How much does it cost?

The bottom rungs are reserved for people, products, and companies who haven't been in business very long and lack a meaningful track record, raving fans, and references.

It's common for ideal prospects to ask themselves questions about a company's years of experience, their product, or their service reviews, references, specialized knowledge, and such. If you've been in business for a while, have a track record of accomplishment, and can show a long list of satisfied clients, then that moves you up a few rungs. You're better off than the startups, but the biggest financial rewards are reserved for those at the top.

Want to know how to get there? Let's take a look at someone who has done it.

Let's examine what it took him to get there, and then I'll share an alternative path that YOU can take, in YOUR industry, that can help you make YOUR MARK in a fraction of the time, with a fraction of the work, and little to no investment other than your time and willingness to share your expertise.

In visiting with Brett, he pointed out that it seems like there is a financial advisor everywhere you look. They're at networking meetings and chamber of commerce meetings, knocking on doors, sending you mailers.... They're everywhere.

Brett also pointed out that Dave Ramsey is a great example of someone in a crowded industry who found a way to rise above the sea of rivals clogging the lower rungs of the Credibility Ladder. Dave positioned himself as an expert and built tribes of followers all over the country who love to listen to the information he provides, gladly pay for it, and more importantly, share it with others in ways that only make his tribe of friends, fans, and followers grow bigger and faster.

The local financial planner in your town and my town who's having to buy breakfasts, lunches, and dinners every day probably spends a small fortune on advertising and marketing and makes tons of phone calls just hoping to get someone who is willing to sit down and listen.

Here's the interesting thing that Brett pointed out to me. The advice that you are likely to get from the average financial planner down the street isn't that different from what Ramsey is out there saying.

Almost all of them tell you to spend less than you make, invest in assets rather than items that don't generate positive cash flow, have a "rainy day" fund for unexpected expenses, etc. So if the product—their advice—isn't that different, why is there such a difference in the demand for their services and the money they make?

Brett likes to tell his clients about how Dave Ramsey went out and created content that people wanted to consume. Dave invested his time and money leveraging traditional media channels in ways that helped him build a brand and his credibility and promote them both. He took his message to the people wherever they were, however he could. He wrote books. He got syndicated on radio stations across the country ... and TV ... and newspapers ... and magazines.

I'm not saying you couldn't do that too if you had the time, patience, and budget.

But those channels, while still popular, aren't as powerful as they used to be. The good news for you is that the ALTERNATIVES TO THOSE MEDIA CHANNELS aren't as expensive AND ... can be every bit as and in some cases more influential than their predecessors.

Becoming Your Own Media Outlet

I was recently visiting with another friend I respect very much for his business acumen and marketing savvy. His name is Scott Kolbe, and he's the president of a local St. Louis marketing and PR firm called KolbeCo (see http://www.KolbeCo.net). He said, "Brands are becoming their own media outlet," and he's right.

Traditional media outlets don't want to hear this, but it's the truth. Even if they hear it, they don't want to admit it.

If you or your company has a story to tell, you don't need a single reporter, much less a bunch of them, to anoint you as worthy of their coverage in order to reach people in your ideal audience. You can go directly to your audience with your story or message and bypass the media all together.

It wouldn't be hard to argue that until recently, the president of the United States had to make an extraordinary effort to cultivate positive relationships with members of the Washington Press Corps. The media had tremendous power to sway public opinion because THEY were the main delivery mechanism for the news. People went through news outlets when they wanted to know what was going on.

I remember watching Jay Carney, the 29th White House Press Secretary, get roasted in front of a group of reporters during the disastrous rollout of the Obamacare website during October of 2013. He just said, "Gotta go," and walked out while reporters were still talking and asking him questions.

The camera I was watching showed a room full of reporters looking around at each other, dumbfounded, confused, and in apparent disbelief that he just walked out on them. They smirked at each other and shook their heads but didn't have the power to do much about it, because the president didn't need them to deliver a message to the people. He could do it just fine without them.

If President Ronald Reagan's White House Press Secretary had treated the White House Press Corps the way Jay Carney did that day, there would have been hell to pay.

Now the president can take a message straight to the people and spread it like wildfire throughout social media channels, mobile phones, tablets, televisions, and computers worldwide and do it in an instant.

Companies are doing it, too. They are recognizing they have a voice and are now learning to amplify it.

Why do you think Jeff Bezos of Amazon.com bought *The Washington Post*?

In the old days, if you wanted to market an energy drink like Red Bull to sports enthusiasts, you would have had to pay television networks and sports franchises a fortune to have your branding and commercials appear during a broadcast of their football, baseball, hockey, or basketball games.

Red Bull visionaries went on to create their OWN extreme sports and events and their OWN venues and produced their OWN video coverage of their unique events that their ideal customers want to watch, discuss, and share. The sporting events they created were designed to appeal to their ideal audience. The video coverage of those events featured Red Bull branding all over the venue as well as the athletes who were competing.

As of the date of this writing, their YouTube channel has millions of subscribers and hundreds of millions of views.

For all intents and purposes, Red Bull didn't just create a YouTube video channel, they created their own network. They have channels featuring water sports, skateboarding, motor sports, BMX biking, and more.

You don't need a budget or a vision as big as the White House, Amazon.com, or Red Bull. You've just got to start somewhere. And you should start now.

Building Your Audience: Old Vs. New

Let's compare the old vs. the new way of building your audience and tribe of friends, fans, and followers.

Mike Koenigs, a San Diego–based thought leader (see http://www.instantcustomer.com) whom we respect very much and who has inspired much of our work, did an amazing job of contrasting the past with the future of media in marketing. I'm paraphrasing a bit here, but he deserves the credit for being the first to point it out—to us, anyway.

In the old days, your goal might have been to appear on as many TV channels as you could. The NEW approach is to get discovered and build an audience on INTERNET VIDEO CHANNELS. YouTube is the most prominent one, but there are lots of others that matter and can help you build your tribes too.

In the old days, your goal might have been to appear on as many radio stations as you could. The NEW approach is to get discovered and build an audience on PODCAST CHANNELS. That way people can download and listen to your podcasts while they are walking, jogging, or lying around the pool.

In the old days, your goal might have been to appear in as many newspapers as you could. The NEW approach is to get discovered and build an audience on ARTICLE POSTING SITES where bloggers, webmasters, newsletter publishers, and others are looking for content they can share with their audiences.

The deal with ARTICLE SITES is that you provide articles that anyone can publish, as long as they credit you as the source and print your bio at the bottom, which often contains your website and contact information. (If you want to see an example of a great article site, see http://www.eZineArticles.com.)

It's a great way to attract ideal prospects, establish your authority, demonstrate your expertise, and get website traffic and leads you wouldn't have gotten otherwise. There are lots of great article posting sites where you can make your content available to publishers and bloggers without spending a dime.

In the old days, your goal might have been to appear in as many magazines as possible. The NEW approach is to get discovered and build an audience on BLOG sites.

In the old days, your goal might have been to get mentions on the newswire of breaking stories. The NEW approach is to get your news directly to the people who are interested in it.

Status sites, like Facebook and Twitter, are where people update what's going on in their lives or businesses in real time. They allow folks to bypass the media and take messages straight to their tribes. There are plenty of these sites that can help you get your messages out quickly and easily as well.

If you think that sounds like a lot of work, you would be right ... but we contend that it's worth it.

Why is it important to embrace, understand, and utilize these new approaches?

Let's talk about that.

Sales Vs. Marketing

For the longest time, I didn't understand the difference between marketing and sales.

Allen Minster is the coauthor of the book *Sales Utopia* (see http://www.frontline-advisors.com) and once told me that marketing was like planting crops in the springtime: you planted your seeds, watered your soil, killed the weeds, and gave them time to grow. Sales, Allen said, was like the harvest.

Unfortunately, salespeople are out trying to harvest where no crop has been planted, or worse... they don't follow up and someone else gets to eat the fruits of their labor.

When I first met Allen, we were sitting at a table at Applebee's and he pulled out his pen and a napkin and explained something to me that I never forgot. I figure I might as well share it with you, too.

Allen drew this little graph and said that for a sale to be made, two things had to happen. Prospects had to be qualified on a scale from zero to ten. What did he mean by qualified? He meant that prospects had to have a need. They had to be able to make a decision, and they had to be able to pay for it.

They also had to be interested.

Allen pointed to the upper right-hand corner of his graph and said that when a rep was in front of a prospect who was highly qualified and highly interested, it was a good use of time, because the probability of a sale was high. If a rep spent time talking with people who weren't both, the rep wasn't a salesperson, just a professional visitor.

Because reps never knew when someone was ready to buy, in the old days, they went out and assembled a database of presumably qualified prospects they assumed were "tens" and began investing dollars in marketing to them, hoping that each contact would move their interest higher and higher until prospects called them when they were ready to buy.

There were only so many ways to reach a prospect, so reps tried to use them all. Reps could stop by, call them on the phone, send them mail—you know, the approaches that just aren't working that well anymore.

The Next Endangered Species: Salespeople?

I'm not convinced that salespeople as we've known them to exist in the past aren't becoming unnecessary to a large degree.

As Allen and I discussed one day, there are really two main reasons why salespeople USED to be necessary. Reason number one was that they had specialized product knowledge. The second reason was that they could give prospects the information they needed about pricing.

Now prospects can get both online. And if you don't think they can find out what your confidential pricing is, then you are being naive. It's a safe bet that someone, posting in a forum somewhere, let the cat out of the bag and your so-called confidential pricing isn't such a secret anymore.

The walls that separate salespeople from their prospects using traditional methods have gotten thicker and taller.

The good news is that you can still mail advertisements to your prospects; the bad news is that they sort them over the trash can.

You can still send emails to prospects, but unless they know who you are and what you want, and know it is something that can interest or assist them, expect your emails to end up in the spam filter.

You can still call a prospect on the phone. Unfortunately, it's not just the receptionist you need to get past to talk to the boss. You have to get past Caller ID, twice, because the receptionist and the boss both have it. And they both know how to use it.

In this day and age, dropping in to see a prospect without an appointment isn't cool or appreciated; in fact, it kind of makes you look desperate.

You can still advertise on radio and TV, but people can switch channels with the push of a button, and with so many people using digital video recorders, most can skim right through the commercials altogether.

Even if you are lucky enough to get someone to pay attention to your ad, the number of people who will actually believe it is far lower than most reps selling you the advertising are likely to admit.

What DO People Trust?

People trust word of mouth ... period.

If you can't figure out a way to become involved in those word-of-mouth conversations when they relate to your products, services, or expertise, then it doesn't really matter how good your products, services, or knowledge is.

Word-of-mouth conversations that used to take place on the telephone and face-to-face are now taking place online at popular social media sites like YouTube, Twitter, Facebook, Pinterest, and others.

Those conversations are taking place in amazing numbers, too. We are talking about hundreds of millions of people ... not only in this country but abroad as well.

There are hundreds of millions of blogs out there, too.

They are effective places to put your content, since people go there to read about things they are interested in learning more about and they don't go there with the expectation of being sold to.

YouTube isn't just one of the most popular search engines. It also doubles as a social network, and it's not just being used by kids who want to see people slipping on banana peels and stuff.

Not long ago, I was having a discussion with a friend who just bought her first home. It was a fixer-upper, and she smiled when she told me that YouTube had easily saved her family over $10,000 since they bought it.

How? She told me she was recently married and her husband didn't know how to fix much of anything. He just wasn't very handy, but there wasn't much he couldn't and didn't learn how to fix by watching YouTube videos. They were able to do tons of work themselves that they would have otherwise had to hire out. They bought the best tools and materials for their jobs without overpaying ... and I hear those types of stories all the time.

People go on YouTube and other search engines to find answers to their questions, to learn how to do something, or to get other people's opinions on products or services they are thinking about buying. They watch videos, share them, and discuss them in ways that help other members of the YouTube community as well.

How big is it? According to YouTube.com's own statistics, they acknowledge over a billion UNIQUE users and over a hundred hours of new content being uploaded every minute, and viewership rates continue to skyrocket.

YouTube isn't the only video channel, either. There are others that count, too, and people aren't just watching videos on their computers. The number of people watching videos on their mobile devices, tablets, and Smart TV's are skyrocketing as well.

Almost everyone has mobile phones, and they take them everywhere with them. Calling them phones is an understatement. They are more like computers, miniature movie cinemas, GPS systems, text message delivery mechanisms, and music players that also happen to make phone calls.

It seems like every time you turn on the television or radio, wireless carriers are bragging about their faster and faster speeds that make Internet streaming on your mobile devices better and better.

According to Pew Internet research, 75% of teenagers text and average about 60 texts a day, making it their most common form of communication.

According to Forrester Research, about 6 billion SMS messages are sent each DAY in the United States alone, and most of them get read within minutes of being received. Videos, pictures, articles, and other links to interesting content are often attached.

Recently, Paul Colligan (see http://www.Colligan.com) contrasted the power of printed brochures and smartphones and was quick to point out one obvious difference: People aren't running around throwing away their smartphones.

What this means to you is that if you know how to provide valuable content and communicate with current and potential customers, when and how they want to be communicated with, using video, mobile text, and other social media technologies, then you have a decided advantage ... period.

Sales = Closing Percentage × Number of Selling Opportunities

Sales has always been a numbers game, and revenue is a result of the number of selling opportunities multiplied by the closing percentage of your sales reps.

Want to know how to maximize both?

Let's talk about the number of selling opportunities.

If 100 people interact with your business each day and you can double that number—closing percentage remaining the same—what should happen to your sales?

They should double, right?

What if there was a way to double, triple, or grow the number of selling opportunities side of that equation into an infinite number, without your having to add staff at proportional levels ... maybe not add any staff at all?

Let's talk about maximizing your closing percentage.

If you're the owner, does anyone know your business better than you? Is anyone more passionate or more invested? What if it were possible to capture your knowledge, passion, and enthusiasm and share it with every single person who came in contact with your business?

What if you could make the perfect presentation of your products, services, and expertise every single time, without fail? What would that do to the closing percentage side of the equation? You can't do better than your best, so it's safe to assume it would be maximized, right?

What's the answer?

It's the use of Internet video. Putting out videos allows you to put your company's best foot forward 24 hours a day, 365 days a year, worldwide so your message can reach an almost unlimited number of people.

In video form, your message is always rock solid and sound, and delivered perfectly. It maximizes your closing percentage because there are no screwups. Web videos don't call in sick, ask for raises, collect commissions, have off days, or run off to start a business competing with you.

Some of you might be thinking that what I'm suggesting is sales and marketing blasphemy.

What about relationships with prospects and clients ... won't they suffer? Consider this and judge for yourself.

I was just hanging out at a sidewalk cafe having dinner with Mark, a high school buddy of mine, in Springfield, Missouri. We were just sitting there, telling lies about the good old days, when "Coach" (a reality TV star from the CBS show *Survivor*) walked by us.

We both recognized him, introduced ourselves, and offered to buy a round if he would tell us stories about being on the show. He was totally cool about it. He sat down. We ordered drinks and visited for about an hour before he went on his way.

Here's the lesson: He seemed like a friend before we ever met him. Mark and I both felt like we knew him before we ever got to say hello. Why? Because we saw him lots of times on TV and video interviews.

Here's the deal: If you use video marketing and YouTube marketing to introduce yourself and your company to your ideal prospects, they can start liking and trusting YOU and YOUR company before they even meet you.

Think about it. Are there any actors or actresses you'd love to meet and have dinner with? Any musicians? Any politicians you couldn't stand to be around? Why? You don't know them ... they're strangers, but you feel like they aren't.

That's the power of video. It's a great way to let people get the chance to know you, in many cases before you ever meet them. It's pretty much like the exact opposite of a cold call.

You might be thinking that you don't want to be on video or wouldn't know what to say.

To address the first problem, it's easy to hire a spokesperson or model so you don't have to be in the video (see http://www.BusinessWebVideos.com).

The second challenge might even be easier to overcome than the first.

If you truly understand your customers' wants, needs, fears, and concerns, then you should know what problems they're trying to solve and what answers they are seeking when they go online. You should also know how to answer each of those questions.

Virtual Marketing, Sales & Customer Service

I'm quick to credit Internet marketer Mike Koenigs (see http://www.InstantCustomer.com) for coming up with the strategy of identifying the ten FAQ's and SAQ's. FAQ stands for Frequently Asked Questions and SAQ stands for the Should Ask Questions, and those are the questions your prospects SHOULD ask if they had the same expertise and experience that you have. And since they don't know what they don't know, you can create for yourself the opportunity to demonstrate superior knowledge, position yourself as an expert, and provide exceptional value they aren't likely to get elsewhere.

Many of your best prospects might not be willing to spend an hour with a salesperson, but they would be willing to watch a couple short videos that tell them exactly what they want to know, fast, so they can make a decision to buy from you or your website.

Additionally, there are more of your best prospects who might hesitate to share their TRUE concerns with a salesperson or their coworkers. And when your videos give them a way to get the answers they need to the REAL important questions surrounding their TRUE concerns without their having to say them out loud, then you won't miss a bunch of sales you would have otherwise made.

Remember the movie *Vacation* with Chevy Chase? After a cross-country trip to his favorite amusement park, Clark Griswold goes BERSERK when he arrives with his dejected family to find out the park is CLOSED from the talking moose standing by the park entrance.

I bet that's how some of YOUR BEST PROSPECTS (and customers) feel when they have questions or need your expertise after hours, when you're closed. They may not go berserk, but they may go and buy from someone else instead of you.

What's the solution? That's easy. Answer their most common questions using business videos on your website. Think of it as your 24-hour sales and service team.

As if you didn't have enough reasons to start using videos as part of your online and social media marketing, consider this:

When videos are done right and the secrets for getting them ranked are put to good use, the search engines love them ... sometimes even more than websites.

(Bonus: See http://www.BusinessWebVideos.com and review the "secret weapons" to learn how to get your videos to rank higher in search engines.)

In the online marketing world, just like in the offline marketing world, timing is everything. As Allen Minster always says, "Your goal is to be in front of your prospects when they're ready to buy."

How to Win Before You Begin

Regardless of whether it's blogs, videos, podcasts, websites, or social media sites, you need to make sure your business is easy to find online.

If it isn't, what can you do about it? The answer is lots of things. But if you don't do one thing first, and do it well, then the rest of the good things you do might not be enough to matter.

It is absolutely imperative that you know what keyword phrases your ideal prospects are typing into search engines when they want what you have to offer.

All the people who AREN'T making money online are sitting around at kitchen tables, conference rooms, and offices asking each other what they think their prospects are typing into search engines to find them.

By comparison, the people who DO know how to market online don't have to guess. They do keyword research in ways that let them KNOW they can win before they even start.

There are some very important things you need to know about those phrases before you decide which ones need to be part of your online marketing strategy.

The first thing you need to know about the potential keyword phrases you are considering as part of your marketing efforts is how many people are typing those words or phrases into search engines every day. It doesn't do any good to build marketing campaigns around phrases that hardly anyone is typing in or intentions that people have in small numbers.

The second thing you need to know about is the quality and quantity of the online competitors who are trying to get their content placed above yours for those same words, phrases, and intentions. Strategically speaking, you have to know if your marketing efforts will pay off BEFORE you launch them.

The third thing you need to know is how RELEVANT those words or phrases are to what you have to offer and the intentions of the people using them in search engines.

Finally, you need to know that there is value, commercially speaking, associated with the best keyword phrases. In other words, is there commercial intent associated with a person typing a phrase into a search engine? Are they likely to spend money on a product or service that gives them what they want or need? There is a big difference in commercial significance between a phrase like "how to get x, y, and z" and a similar phrase like "how to get x, y, and z for free."

Once you've successfully performed keyword research and created content that answers the frequently asked questions and the should ask questions, you embed the most valuable keyword phrases throughout your content in ways that appeal to the search engines as much as the answers appeal to the people looking for them.

Then you are ready to start marketing.

(Bonus: See http://www.BusinessWebVideos.com and review the "secret weapons" if you want to know what our favorite KEYWORD RESEARCH tool/web application is and how you can use it to eliminate a bunch of your guesswork and spot important trends you otherwise would have missed.)

Jug Fishing = Internet Marketing

The next question is, how? It's easy to get confused and overwhelmed, so maybe this will help.

It's a lot like jug fishing ... and if you don't know what that is, don't feel bad; neither did I until recently.

I have a friend named Matt who grew up by a river in Alabama and had ADD when he was a little kid. He told me about his first fishing trip with his dad. Once they got there and got all set up and had the fishing line in the water, they sat ... and sat ... and sat, waiting for the fish to bite and the bobber to go under water so Matt could reel in a fish.

It was a horrible experience for the fidgety little kid who couldn't sit still waiting for one fishing line to get some action. It wasn't much fun for his dad either, who was just trying to have a nice day with his little boy.

The next time—and there was a next time—Matt's dad changed his strategy and came up with an idea that changed everything. He decided to teach Matt about jug fishing.

Jug fishing is when you get a bunch of empty plastic milk jugs and tie a line and hook to each of them. Because fish swim at different depths, it is important to use different lengths of line. You put bait on the hooks and drop them in the water where you know there are lots of fish and where nobody else is fishing. Once Matt got to jug fish, he was running up and down the riverbank all day trying to keep up with all the fish they were catching.

Here's what jug fishing has to do with online marketing.

The river is the Internet. The fish are your prospects. The keyword research process is like having a fishing guide who knows all the secrets about all the spots where nobody else is fishing and there are plenty of fish. The jugs and lines are like your media channels. The content you put out is your bait, and it is important to put out fresh content for the same reason it makes sense to put out fresh bait: You want to attract rather than repel your ideal targets. A fishing net that scoops up the fish while they're hooked is like a lead capture or landing page process that gathers your prospects' names and automatically follows up with them in exchange for a special report or offer of some sort that you've made available to them.

If you've got a website, it's like fishing with one line in the water. If you are catching enough fish one at a time from your site, then you don't need to jug fish; if not, why not put out thousands of them everywhere your ideal prospects can be found congregating online?

Here's a secret: Sooner or later, you're going to have to learn how to do this anyway. You might as well start sooner.

You have two choices.

You can do a lot of work for a little impact or you can do a little work for a lot of impact. What separates the two choices? The first is strategic integration of your efforts. The second is automation.

When you take a jug fishing approach to online marketing, you will find that the whole of your effort is greater than the sum of the parts. When you strategically integrate the creation and distribution of your blog posts, videos, articles, podcasts, and other forms of content, your presence gets amplified ... in some cases exponentially.

Automate & Dominate

When you automate content distribution, one person using the right tools can accomplish more and better results than an entire marketing department in a fraction of the time.

For example, let's say you want to automate the distribution of your content, which, if done manually, is a boring and time-consuming task that will drive your staff to quit their jobs or at least quit doing this task. Let me explain an alternative that leverages technology and automation.

Let's pretend that you created a piece of content that answered a frequently asked question and you wanted to distribute it to all of the online sites that mattered most, in video format, podcast format, blog format, status site format (like updates in places like Facebook and Twitter), and article format. Let's pretend that you wanted to update the social bookmarking sites as well.

This is how you would do it.

Create a video and check the video sites you want it to get uploaded onto along with your keyword-loaded titles, tags, and descriptions. Press a button and let automated systems log on and load up those sites with your videos automatically. Save yourself hours of work EVERY TIME you put out new content—which, if you're doing it right, will be often.

Then, by changing a few words in your video script, you could create a blog post, and with the touch of another button, you can let automated systems log on and load up those sites with your blogs automatically.

You could do the same thing with a bunch of article sites and status sites as well.

Of course, your automated systems could distribute your content through podcast channels and update your social bookmarking sites as well.

That's strategic integration and automation. That's how the best online marketers dominate their online space. This process is absolutely an unfair advantage and explains in large part why business owners and marketers are exercising in futility when they think all they need to do is start a blog, Facebook page, or Twitter account and post some decent content once in a while.

Anyone can do that stuff, and if you focus your time and energy on tasks that anyone and everyone can do, you forfeit any potential advantages you could otherwise have by leveraging strategic integration and automation that everyone else can't or doesn't do.

(Bonus: See http://www.BusinessWebVideos.com and review the "secret weapons" to learn what tool we use to automate our content distribution processes.)

There are two reasons you want to dominate search engines for your keyword phrases.

One is so you can be found by your ideal prospects when they are looking for your services. The other is to clog spaces and rankings so your competitors DON'T get found.

Getting found online is one thing. Making sure you are found by your IDEAL prospects can be an entirely different matter. Here's something you might not have thought of.

Bob Levinstein is the president of CruiseCompete (see http://www.CruiseCompete.com), and prior to his current venture, he started a company that became one of the top five online recruiting companies in the country. He asked me, "What's the worst thing that can happen if you pay to advertise for one of your company's job openings?" I quickly answered, "Nobody responds." He said, "Nice try, but that's the second worst thing that could happen."

He said, "The WORST thing that could happen is that your company could get flooded with applicants, none of which are qualified to do the job, and you have to waste a ton of additional time and resources sorting through them all before you find out that you can't hire any of them."

When you market correctly online, you can solve problems before they occur, seize opportunities others overlook, and avoid getting bogged down in resource-intensive activities that won't produce results.

Keyword phrases help sort and sift prospects.

Twitter: Introductions, Curiosity & the Law of Attraction

I used to think Twitter was stupid. Probably because I didn't understand all the reasons it was so relevant. I didn't care where Paris Hilton had dinner. I didn't care what kind of shoes the Kardashians just purchased. It seemed stupid and I didn't get it.

I get it now and could talk for hours about ways to use Twitter to build your brand and demonstrate your subject matter expertise, but I want to take just a minute to explain how you can use it to attract and engage more of your ideal prospects.

If someone follows you on Twitter, what's the first thing you want to know? Who are they and why are they following you, right? Guess what? Almost everyone else feels the same way. What does that mean to you?

It means that you need a way to get introduced to fun, knowledgeable, and active Twitter users who share your passions and value your expertise—as many of them as possible, as fast as you can.

Let me give you an example. Let's pretend that you offer products or services that you sell primarily to human resource directors at companies all over the world. How could you use Twitter to build a tribe of followers consisting of those types of people?

One of the easiest ways is to identify influential Twitter users who already have a tribe of people following them that you would like to have following you.

Have you ever heard of a lady named China Gorman? Unless you are a senior level human resources practitioner, the answer is probably no.

Why? It is because a few years ago, she was the chief operating officer for the Society of Human Resource Management, or SHRM as it's also known, which is the largest association of human resource professionals in the world with over 200,000 members worldwide.

Since the CEO had the highest visibility and was the one most often in the spotlight, that meant that the only people who would be likely to know who China was or care what she thought about anything would be who? It would be senior level HR people, right?

So, if you looked her up on Twitter, you might find out that she has a few thousand followers. The next thing you could do would be to gather all her followers and start to follow them.

Why? It's so they can ask the obvious question, "Who are you and why are you following them?" A good percentage will read your profile bio, take a look at some of your recent tweets, maybe click on the link to your site, and make a decision as to whether or not you share common interests or complementary knowledge to the point that they would be willing to follow you, too.

If your tweets, profile, and website seem relevant and interesting, you may get anywhere from 10% to 30% of the people you followed to follow you back.

It's not totally about how much money you have or how big your corporation is, either. If you are thinking that you couldn't share your knowledge with a tribe of followers that rivals or exceeds your industry giants, I would encourage you to think again.

Using the exact same strategy I just shared with you, I was able to build multiple Twitter accounts that ranked in the top 1% in the world. More importantly, these tools and strategies allowed me to get my ideas introduced to hundreds of new people EACH DAY on EACH of my Twitter accounts, and they can for you, too.

Can you use Twitter to get introduced to more of the right people? Yes. Can you use it to share your ideas with them quickly, easily, and without spending a bunch of money? Yes. Can you demonstrate social proof that you are an expert and others see value in your knowledge? Yes.

A friend of mine just tried to get a book published. One of the first questions the publishing company asked her was how many Twitter followers she had.

Why? Because they wanted proof that there was some sort of interest, an established demand, and a mechanism that could make viral marketing of a new book possible.

* Warning: Read Twitter's Terms of Service and abide by them. Excessive following and/or unfollowing of Twitter accounts can get your account suspended. I know this from experience. :)

YouTube: Introductions, Curiosity & the Law of Attraction

Tribe building on YouTube is fairly similar, strategically speaking.

Like Twitter, YouTube is a search engine AND a social network. Far too many people fail to realize the power of YouTube beyond the availability of great videos. There is a whole networking element whereby people can subscribe to your YouTube channel and share videos and discuss videos with their online friends or contacts in the YouTube network.

The strategy is very similar to the one you use with Twitter. Instead of following someone on YouTube, like you do on Twitter, your introduction comes in the form of contact requests.

Who do you send contact requests to on YouTube? One way to start is by gathering lists of usernames of people who are commenting on and discussing certain topics and videos.

For example, if you wanted to get introduced on YouTube to business owners or executives, then you might consider looking up videos on Harvard Business Review's channel and gathering the usernames of people who comment on them. Send them contact requests and let them check you out and decide if they want to accept or not.

(Bonus: See http://www.BusinessWebVideos.com and review the "secret weapons" to discover the online application we use that AUTOMATICALLY gathers targeted YouTube usernames AND sends them contact requests.)

Sorting Vs. Convincing: Work With the Willing

It's possible that you might be thinking that an audience-building/introductory approach like what I'm suggesting won't work for you or that people might get mad if you reach out to them and take the initiative to introduce yourself online.

Of course I do get comments from random people every once in a while who tell me to take a long walk off a short pier, go pound sand, or die, but they are by FAR the exception rather than the rule.

My goal and your goal should be the same, and that is to work with those who are willing.

Look ... anything is possible, and you can't please everybody. But if you put out good content that is relevant and helpful to people who share your interests and value your expertise, then doors can open up to you that are closed to others.

The purpose of putting out great content is to get found by your ideal prospects, wherever they hang out online. The goal of great content is to ATTRACT more buyers, establish credibility, and create desire for what you do or offer.

Once you've got a prospect's attention, how do you turn them into actual leads? How do you CAPTURE their contact information? That's easy. You offer them something of significant value that is relevant to their wants and needs and has enough of a perceived value that your ideal prospects will gladly give you their contact information—phone number, email, name, etc.—to get it.

It could be a free special report, an instructional video series, or a 30-day trial of one of your most popular services. People who are struggling with problems value solid advice, special offers, and recommendations that save them time and money and protect them from unnecessary hassles.

I saw an interview between Anthony Robbins and Russell Brunson not long ago, and Russell made a comment that hit me between the eyes and I never forgot it. He said, "A confused customer always says no."

That's why I'm a huge fan of having a simple lead capture process. Some people call it a lead capture page, a squeeze page, or a landing page. Basically it's a mini-website that asks people if they have certain problems and offers them solutions, special offers, and insight into how to solve those problems in exchange for their contact information. (See http://www.buildatribe.com for an example of what a mini-site looks like and does.)

It separates buyers from browsers. It's not about showcasing your brand or the technical specifications of your products or becoming an online e-commerce storefront. That's what your MAIN website is for. The purpose of your mini-site is MUCH more specific. It's to capture leads in exchange for a specific offering.

So if you create great content and distribute it everywhere to ATTRACT your prospects ...

And you use special offers and mini-sites to CAPTURE their contact information ...

What's the last step? How do you CONVERT them into clients?

The answer is AUTOMATED FOLLOW-UP. Once you know who your prospects are, specifically, AND you know they are interested in what you offer (otherwise they wouldn't have given you their contact info), then you need to stay in touch with them and continue educating them about all the additional ways they can solve their problems and seize opportunities they would otherwise miss without you, your products, or your services. Send them emails. Send them texts. Send them videos. And send them regularly.

How long should people stay in your database?

As long as they don't opt out from receiving your communications, the answer to that one is easy: forever.

The Online Land Rush: Act Now

So, when should you start? That's up to you. But here's some food for thought.

According to Wikipedia,

> Sooners is the name given to settlers in the midwest of the United States who entered the Unassigned Lands in what is now the state of Oklahoma before President Grover Cleveland officially proclaimed them open to settlement on March 2, 1889.
>
> Problems with Sooners continued with each successive land run; in an 1895 land run as much as half of the available land was taken by Sooners.

In other words, when it became apparent that free land was going to be made available for settlement, lots of folks went out early, scouted the best land, and hid in ditches or whatever they had to do to be there first the moment the land was made available for settlement. Everyone else got the leftovers.

In Internet marketing terms, there is a new frontier and it is already open for settlement. People just don't realize it yet or know how to make their claims.

Knowing what you know now, if you could go back in time and had the chance to claim whatever land you wanted, anything west of the Mississippi River for the sake of discussion, what kind of land would you pick? Would you select lakefront properties, oceanfront properties, mountaintop views? You bet. Why? Because you know in advance what land is the most valuable, right?

We're not saying the Internet is going to get used up; that's nonsense. But what we are going to say is that the online property surrounding profitable keyword phrases and intentions that attract lots of buyers and few competitors (or good ones anyway), and that are relevant and have lots of commercial value, THOSE aren't going to sit around forever.

The longer you wait, the harder and more expensive it will be to stake your claim on that Internet space. Of course, you'll always have the option of taking whatever is left over and has been picked through by everyone else, but you don't have to.

You are right here, right now, for a reason. We doubt it's an accident. We commend you.

Your understanding of this powerful process and the amazing tools that automate and execute it for you can serve you very well, in almost any endeavor, regardless of whether you're working for yourself or somebody else, for a very long time.

It's kind of like having a superpower and unfair advantage over others who don't. But he who has the power and doesn't use it is no better off than anyone else. Are you going to be the one with the superpower or be just like everyone else?

Shortly after I got married, I started a business. Like most entrepreneurs, I struggled for the first few years. At one point, my wife asked me, "How long are you going to keep doing this?" I looked her in the eye and told her, "Until it works."

She wanted a deadline. "How about 6 months? A year? Really? How long are you going to keep this up?" I gave her the same answer: "Until it works."

If you're an entrepreneur, you know that you have to be committed to the outcomes you want, relentless about making forward progress. It helps to be resourceful and flexible in your approaches, but you must always be committed.

I believe you should feel the same way about building your business online that you feel about building it offline.

Because we want you to get what you want sooner rather than later and suffer less than is necessary in the pursuit of your goals, we decided to dedicate the rest of this book to sharing the most common mistakes we see others make.

Often one solution, executed well, will solve many problems. At the risk of sounding repetitive, we're going to point them out anyway so that we can keep adding to the pile of reasons WHY you should take the actions that are necessary.

Remember, we didn't write this book so you would just read it. We wrote it because we actually want you to take action and do amazing things.

Section 2: 89 of the Best Ways to Attract, Capture & Convert Prospects Online (& Offline) *(Hint: Don't make the same mistakes.)*

Mistake 1: Failing to Love the Haters

What should you do about people online who want to discredit you and your ideas? Undoubtedly, you have competitors with a vested interest in damaging you and your reputation online. You could also be the target of ignorant and bored people who think it is fun to go online and disparage others.

Either way, if you are trying to create an online presence using new media and social media tools to establish your authority as a subject matter expert online, then you will need to know how to deal with these people.

Sure, you can delete their negative comments or set up your social media account profiles to screen their comments before they get posted, but is that the best way to handle it? The answer might be no.

At a conference in San Diego recently, I had the opportunity to visit with Paul Colligan (see http://www.Colligan.com), who is best known for his expertise in online marketing. I told him about TestMyTeen.com, a company that sells home drug tests and home drug test kits online to parents.

As you can imagine, there are all kinds of people, drug users in particular, who don't consider the similarities between a parent looking at a report card to MAKE SURE their kids are doing well in school and parents looking at the results of a drug test at home to MAKE SURE their kids are living a drug-free lifestyle.

Comments directed at TestMyTeen.com's Facebook page, YouTube channel, and blogs are often less than complimentary. Paul didn't see this as an obstacle. He saw it as an opportunity.

What better social proof could TestMyTeen.com possibly put on display than a bunch of critics arguing about why it's no big deal for kids to experiment with drugs? Let critics argue that a 12-year-old's "right to privacy" in their PARENTS' home should outweigh things like the legal and health dangers of heroin use, cocaine use, or possession.

If parents had any doubt about how accessible drugs were to their kids or how little fear of consequences so many kids have regarding drugs, what better way to show them than to let them see it for themselves.

The more TestMyTeen.com's opponents try to discredit their video content on social media sites, the more the critics demonstrate the importance of their services.

Based on that discussion with Paul, there may be plenty of incidents where it is best to put out lots of content fully expecting that it will start conversations and discussions online. Love the hate and resist the urge to silence your critics online. You might end up turning your adversaries into allies.

Mistake 2: Cold-Calling Prospects Who Should Be Calling You

If you're trying to build your business and you get your first opportunity to speak with a potential client, which question would you prefer they ask you? Is this a cold call? Or: Are you the person I've seen in all the videos?

If you've made quality online videos with valuable content, then you have created two significant advantages. Number one, you have positioned yourself as a subject matter expert and proven your expertise. Number two, you have created built-in rapport and trust.

Your audience members will be much more likely to trust what you have to say because you've already shown them that your ideas have been valuable in the past. Additionally, if you've made videos that showcased your personality along with your valuable content, then you've already created connections and bonds with all kinds of people you've never met.

If you're one of those who loves to cold-call and doesn't ever want to stop cold-calling, then don't let me discourage you. Go get 'em, tiger.

If you're not and would only like to spend your time helping people who want your help and appreciate your expertise, then put your thoughts, ideas, and insights on videos ... and share them.

Mistake 3: Failure to Let the Message and/or Product Be the Star When Using Web Videos

It happens all the time. Some owners want the limelight. They want to "star" in all their company's sales, service, and training videos. Or they select a hotshot employee to do it for them.

Here's another idea. Let the message and/or product be the star. What if the owner's personality, style, or image doesn't appeal to the key demographics of the ideal prospect or customer? What if the hotshot employee quits and goes to work for a competitor? Do you want all your company's videos and its online personality associated with someone who NOW works for a competitor?

Mistake 4: Failure to Eliminate Resistance Before It Occurs

Have you ever walked up to a complete stranger and had them look at you like, "Hey, don't I know you from somewhere?" or better yet, "Hey, I know you!" or "I'm a fan of your work."?

It happens to me all the time. Why? Because I understand the power of Internet video. I use web video for more than just YouTube marketing. I use online video marketing as part of my website marketing strategy, email marketing campaigns, mobile marketing campaigns, Internet branding, and social media marketing tools as well.

I love walking into meetings with business owners I've never met and having them smile and greet me like a friend they've known for years. It's always fun to hear them say, "Hey, you're the guy on the videos," or "I already know what you do and want you to help us do it, too!"

It's hard to find a better way to build trust and rapport and educate prospects before meeting them than referrals, videos, or videos shared by referrals.

Mistake 5: Showcasing Bad Grammar, Punctuation, and Spelling (or Not Putting Out Content Because of It)

Want to know one of the biggest advantages of using online video? It covers up your flaws.

Which ones? Well, in my case, there are plenty, particularly when it comes to spelling and punctuation. Fortunately for me, those skills (or lack thereof) aren't on display when I'm sharing helpful ideas on video.

The nice thing about video marketing is that you get to talk with your audience and let them focus on the important things, like the quality of your ideas and your passion, rather than whether or not you have a goofy comma in the right place or not.

Plus, since what you put on the Internet seems to last forever and isn't easily erased, it makes sense to do everything you can to put your best foot forward. Viral marketing is great when paired with good content. It causes problems when the content is embarrassing. Why take unnecessary risks?

If you insist on putting out text-based content, it might be worth it to hire proofreaders.

Mistake 6: Failure to Point Out Benefits

My son Clayton and I went out for dinner the other night and I asked him to pick whatever restaurant he wanted to go to. He said he was in the mood for some roast beef and he decided we should go to Lion's Choice.

As we were walking into the building, there was a beautifully designed sign on the glass door that said, "Follow Louie on Twitter & Facebook." I was left to assume that Louie the Lion was their mascot. I was also left to wonder, "Why I should follow him on Twitter and Facebook?" Do you know why?

It's simple. They gave me no reason to follow Louie. As much as I like the roast beef sandwiches they sell, I have no idea why I should take the time to do that. Their marketing people forgot to let me know what was in it for me, and until they tell me the benefits I will receive if I do, I won't be following them on Twitter, Facebook, or YouTube. Don't make the same mistake.

When someone lands on your video channel, make sure you take advantage of the trailer video option, because it allows you to welcome visitors to your channel, explain the value of your content to them, and invite them to subscribe so they get future videos as soon as they come out.

Mistake 7: Leaders Driving Slow in the Fast Lane

Have you ever been on the highway and noticed a driver in the passing lane who just won't pass the car in the right lane or get out of the way? Sometimes, it seems like they stay there forever and are totally oblivious to their surroundings and unaware of the long line of cars behind them that can't get past.

I believe there are a whole bunch of senior sales and marketing executives who were EXTREMELY successful but who have absolutely no idea what to do right now to grow their businesses OTHER than MORE of what they've done in the past. They made lots of money and got comfortable. They ignored or didn't understand the importance of market shifts created by the Internet. They failed to immerse themselves in learning new and relevant strategies related to social media marketing, online marketing, video marketing, mobile marketing, and email marketing.

What are these senior sales and marketing executives doing right now? They are clogging the passing lane and holding their companies back. They are demanding more work and sacrifice from the people working hard below them. They are blaming and replacing their subordinates, too. When they run out of people to blame, they update their résumé and go to another company and the cycle is likely to repeat itself.

Some business owners, particularly entrepreneurs, are in the same rut. Because they own the business, they can drive slow in the fast lane for as long as they want, or as long as the market will allow. Employees who value their jobs keep their mouths shut and do what they're told, at least until they can find a different job.

It doesn't have to be that way. Don't be the one driving slow in the fast lane. If you have leaders working for you who won't move out of the way, call them on it. Encourage them to develop additional skills, knowledge, and talented people around them. Remember that you don't have to understand how every technology works in order to use it to your advantage.

Like it or not, change is a constant. It's right behind you, and it is honking and flashing its lights in your rearview mirror. It's up to you to decide if you want to speed up, move over and let others pass, or stop driving completely. It is your choice to embrace change or ignore it. It is not slowing down and it is not going away. Proceed wisely.

Mistake 8: Failing to Begin With the Ideal Outcome in Mind

When it comes to social media marketing, online marketing, email marketing, mobile marketing, text marketing, and linking it all together, I know it can be tempting to jump right in. I know some of you are thirsty for new business, but if you think you can stick your head right into all of it at once, it's going to be like trying to drink from a fire hose or fire hydrant and you're probably going to wish you didn't. You might drown.

Let me encourage you to begin with the end in mind. What's your main goal? Is it to communicate your ideas as inexpensively as possible in ways that attract more of your ideal clients? Is it to capture leads? Is it to convert potential customers into clients? Is it to get feedback on your products and services so you can make necessary improvements without spending a fortune on research and development?

Pick your main goal, and then secure the tools and create the online and social media strategies and tools you need to achieve them. Then identify your second goal and your third and so on. You don't eat an elephant in one sitting, you do it one bite at a time. You don't drink water from a hydrant or fire hose either. There's no reason to get overwhelmed if you do it one step at a time and do it right.

Mistake 9: Ignoring the Warning Signs

What advice would you give if someone you knew was driving down a dead-end street or a road where the bridge was out ahead and they didn't see the signs?

What would you do if they said, "Thanks for your concern, but do you know how long I planned this trip? Do you know how much money I've spent or have any idea how long I've been driving?"

Can you imagine telling someone the bridge is out and having them look at you and say that they've been on this route a hundred times and made it to the other side every time and that they saw the bridge recently and it looked just fine ... and then proceed down the same old road?

When I talk to people about new marketing options offered by social media marketing, online marketing, video marketing, email marketing, and text message marketing, I feel the same way when they tell me, "Yeah, but ..." and then go on to tell me about how successful the old ways of doing things have been in the past even though they're not working so well now.

Some people are hard to help. I want to encourage you to not become one of them. Pay attention to the signs around you. They are not always as obvious as the road signs you pass by every day, but sometimes they ARE and seem impossible to miss, unless you aren't paying attention.

Are fewer people calling your business or buying your products and services? Are you spending more money on marketing and getting worse results? Are you attracting fewer of your ideal prospects? Are your salespeople working harder but delivering more excuses than sales? If so, these are signs, and choosing to ignore them puts you and your business in great peril. Slow down, stop, and change direction.

Jumping your car over the river when the bridge is out only happens in the movies. In real life, and in business ... not so much.

Mistake 10: Lack of Focus on Genuine, Unique, and Authentic Content

So everybody's telling you that you've gotta be on Facebook, LinkedIn, and other social media sites if you want to market your products and services online. Are they right?

The answer is yes ... and no. Yes, because people can't learn about you or buy from you if they don't know you exist. If your competitors are getting found online and you aren't, then you have given them an advantage.

The answer is no if you aren't offering anything unique or valuable on a regular basis. The only thing worse than doing nothing is doing something lame, embarrassing, or damaging to your company or personal reputation.

When talking about online marketing, email marketing, video marketing, and article marketing, establishing a presence on social media marketing sites is a good start, but to really stand out, you need to offer valuable ideas, knowledge, and insights that establish you as an expert and that help people solve problems, and you have to do it in a fun and/or interesting way.

It's not like you can just say, "Let's do some Facebook marketing, or some Youtube marketing, or some Twitter marketing," and expect that more business will come your way.

Just like in the offline world, you have to stand out, and you aren't likely to get ahead if you're just doing what everyone else is doing. Be yourself. Share your unique perspectives. Tell your stories and the lessons you've learned from them.

Content is king—that's no secret. Want to know where your best content is going to come from? Here are some tips and ideas.

Make a list of some of your biggest and best accomplishments, the things that you are most proud of, and they don't have to be things that others even know about. Go crazy, make it a long list, and don't limit yourself. It can go back to things you accomplished as a kid—in sports, in school, at home, wherever.

Often, you will find that as you reflect upon your biggest accomplishments, you will remember facing significant roadblocks or seemingly insurmountable obstacles just prior to overcoming them. What were those obstacles? List them. Describe them. Tell others how you overcame them and what you learned.

Authentic, genuine content that people can relate to, understand, and learn from is the kind that will set you apart, and if you don't share the best of what you have to offer, then neither will the people you send it to.

Mistake 11: Putting the Cart Before the Horse

What is the purpose of your website? What is it supposed to accomplish? What is your objective? Have you ever thought about it? Do you know ... specifically?

What I'm amazed by is the number of people who can't answer the most basic of questions. What is the purpose of your website? I get answers like "I just need to be on the web" or "I need to have a place that tells people about my company" all the time.

If you think the conversation should be focused on how pretty your site is and what color font looks best, then that's fine AFTER you've figured out what the primary purpose of your site is and are accomplishing it.

I want to know if your site attracts, captures, and converts leads into orders. Does it make you money? Does it process orders and ship your products in ways that save you and your employees money? Until you have THOSE objectives identified and your online systems have been built to accomplish those objectives, I encourage you to exercise restraint in your online marketing efforts. As my parents used to say, your cart might be in front of your horse.

Mistake 12: Being Sterile, Politically Correct, and Forgettable

A good traffic accident will clog traffic for hours in a big city. Why? Because everybody wants to see the damage and drama if there is any. When there is nothing unusual or interesting, people drive on by.

If you want your online content to get ignored or forgotten quickly, then stick with politically correct or sterile content.

I'm not suggesting that you manufacture outrage or say ignorant or insensitive things for the shock value alone. Authenticity, or lack thereof, is transparent.

If something sucks, say so. Tell people why and what needs to be done to fix it. Don't hold back. Your audience will know if you do.

The law of attraction is on steroids online. Do what you do best and like to do most. You will attract more of your ideal clients and repel the ones you don't want if you simply give yourself permission to be genuine and share your real thoughts and feelings.

Mistake 13: Bragging

When I'm online, do you know what makes me cringe, just before I click and move on to something else?

It's when I start watching a video or reading an article, blog post, or tweet that talks about how the author's company does this, or that, or how many years they've been in business.

Here's the bottom line: Practically nobody cares.

However, that doesn't stop well-intentioned business owners and marketing folks from blabbering on about how great they are and driving away the very people they want to engage.

Instead, your content had better be focused on one of two things: solving problems or sharing opportunities that will help the people you want to reach.

Quit talking about how great you think you are and start talking about things that can make your clients, friends, and prospects great instead. You'll be glad you did.

Mistake 14: Failure to Make Your Fans Part of Your Creative Process and Product/Service Development

I grew up listening to the hair bands of the 1980s. If I had invested what I spent on cassette tapes, CDs, and concert tickets, then I'd probably have enough set aside to get my son through a good portion of his college education.

So when *That Metal Show* on VH1 comes on, I enjoy finding out what happened to some of my favorite bands years later. I saw an episode the other day where the host, Eddie Trunk, was visiting with Stephen Pearcy, the lead singer of the band Ratt. Back in the day, Ratt could easily play to tens of thousands of adoring fans on any given weekend. Eddie asked Stephen what he was currently working on.

Stephen said that he was doing what he loved the most and that was making music. This time around Stephen didn't seem to be as focused on lasers, pyrotechnics, and colossal stage shows as he was on making music his most diehard fans would enjoy listening to as much as he enjoyed creating it.

Here's what I found interesting. Stephen has a tribe of followers and diehard fans and he interacts with them on a regular basis. He shares his ideas and songs in their preliminary form and asks for fans' feedback on what they like and don't like, and why.

Everybody wins. Stephen puts out music he likes and that his biggest fans want. His followers feel like they are part of his creative process, because they are. He isn't wasting his time or talent on efforts that miss the mark.

Now bands like Ratt are using social media marketing, text marketing, video marketing, and tools like Twitter, Facebook, and YouTube to share opinions, ideas, and content back and forth.

If a lead singer from a rock band who was past his prime twenty years ago can use social media and interaction with his tribe of followers to do more of what he does best and likes to do most, why can't you?

Who are your fans? Are you reaching out to them? Are you listening to them when they reach out to you? Are they part of your product development or market research efforts?

If not, perhaps that's why you haven't reached rock star status in your industry. If you are connecting with fans, then keep it up and rock on!

Mistake 15: Snubbing Your Fan Club

When I was growing up, my friend Doug Pierce joined the Kiss Army. For those of you who didn't grow up in the '70s and '80s, the Kiss Army was the fan club for the hard rock 'n' roll band Kiss.

If I remember correctly, Doug filled out a form and mailed it in with $5 or so and waited in anticipation for 4-6 weeks for his fan club packet to arrive.

When it did arrive in the mail, it had all kinds of pictures and memorabilia. Doug was just as excited to show us all that stuff as we were to see it.

Nowadays, anyone can have a fan club, even you. And you don't have to be a rock star, actor, or famous person. Just as musicians work hard to put out and share their songs, videos, pictures, blogs, and articles, you can put out your ideas, insights, and experience in many of those forms, too. If you do, then you can, and likely will, attract a crowd of people who appreciate you for who you are and what you know.

It won't cost them $5 and they won't have to wait 4-6 weeks to hear from you, either. Your fan club can tune in to you easily, quickly, and often if you just invite them to follow your social media accounts.

You don't need a posse, hype men, or public relations teams, either. What do you need? You need an active social media presence in places like YouTube, Twitter, Pinterest, and Facebook where you regularly share opinions and knowledge and respond to your fans' questions when they ask them.

Be helpful. Be nice. Be there, often. If you do, then watch your fan club online grow. Don't abandon, ignore, or snub them. They are your fans, and they have the power to attract or repel others just like them.

Mistake 16: Only Knocking Down One Pin (Failing to Put Out Content in Multiple Places in Multiple Formats)

Do you know why I and many others think bowling is so cool, even though many of us aren't very good at it? I like the idea of rolling one ball and knocking down lots of pins.

The idea that I can achieve multiple goals with the same effort that it takes to accomplish one goal is one that I try to apply to all my Internet marketing, social media marketing, video marketing, and email marketing endeavors. Everyone knows that creating original content that is valuable is time-consuming.

Here's where most people mess up. They will take the time to develop and share a valuable idea and then post it on their blog. But that's all they do. This is just like rolling one bowling ball and knocking down one pin.

That same idea could also be put out on video and distributed to numerous video sites. It could be polished into an article format with very little extra effort and distributed to article posting sites. It could be turned into a podcast and distributed to podcast channels. Hit the social bookmarking sites and status sites like Twitter and Facebook pages with that same idea and it's like bowling a strike while others are only knocking down one pin.

The bottom line is this: If you are going to take the time to create an original and useful piece of content, make sure you prepare it in multiple formats and distribute it widely. Make one effort and accomplish multiple goals.

Mistake 17: Failure to Capture Leads and Follow Up

A friend of mine has invested a significant portion of his career in the field of mobile marketing. If you've ever gone to a big public event or festival and seen the big fancy trucks with interactive displays promoting various products or services, then that is the kind of work I'm talking about.

The companies he worked for spent tons of money and time to promote specific brands, products, and services. He told me that millions of people had toured their mobile marketing exhibits, and I'll give you one guess as to what happened next.

Absolutely nothing. The displays gathered not one single name or email address. There were no email auto-responders or any other kind of offline or online follow-up system in place to continually communicate the value of their propositions or make special offers either.

His clients had figured out how to get discovered, but failed to capture important contact data. They also failed to have a system in place to convert those prospects into customers.

As my first coauthor Allen Minster always says when it comes to marketing, "If you're going to pay for it, you better figure out a way to get paid for it." So if you don't have a way to capture leads or a way to follow up consistently and turn them into customers, don't waste your money until you do.

Mistake 18: Failing to Sell What's Free

Want more leads from your social media marketing, email marketing, and other Internet marketing efforts? If so, here is something to think about.

In Seth Godin's book *Free Prize Inside,* he talks about the importance of giving things away to potential customers. There are lots of reasons to give people your valuable ideas and other stuff for free. It eliminates prospects' perceived levels of risk, and it generates word-of-mouth referrals, useful feedback, positive feelings, and often future orders.

I was visiting with a friend of mine named Russ Henneberry, who is a content marketing expert in St. Louis, Missouri, and an active social media marketing, online marketing, and email marketing thought leader whom I respect very much (see http://www.ContentMeasures.com).

Russ says, "You have to sell free." It's not enough to just give valuable things away. People pay with their time, and they are asking themselves if your offer is worth it.

If you don't explain the benefits of your free offer, then they won't know it's worth it and many won't bother to take you up on it. If it sounds too good to be true without an explanation of why it makes sense, then many won't bother to take you up on it.

Special offers have been around forever. People expect you will follow up with them if they provide their name and email in exchange for something you offer them at no charge. If the benefits aren't good enough or explained well, then they aren't likely to give you their contact information.

So if you want to attract and capture more leads online, be sure to communicate the benefits of your offer, even if it is something you are giving away for free.

Mistake 19: Failing to Educate, Entertain, or Inspire

If your online marketing and social media marketing content doesn't do at least one of three things, you are likely to repel the very people you want most to attract. I don't care if you are video marketing, article marketing, Facebook marketing, Twitter marketing, or blog marketing.

There was another time I was visiting with Russ (Henneberry) when he opined that content must provide value in at least one of three ways. Before you post comments or content online, you should ask these questions:

Does your content educate people?

Does your content entertain people?

Does your content inspire people?

If the answer to those three questions is no, then you may be wasting your time and resources creating and sharing content online that isn't going to help you. I think Russ is right. So the more you can do to educate, entertain, and inspire your intended audience, the better.

Mistake 20: Location, Location, Location

When trying to buy or sell a home, any good realtor will tell you that value is tied to one thing: location, location, location.

One brick-and-mortar business can succeed while an identical one fails because of where the two are located. Even though they offer the same products, services, and pricing, if one business attracts a high volume of ideal customers and the other one doesn't, then it can succeed while the other fails.

The same principles apply in the arena of Internet marketing and online marketing as the ones in the offline, brick-and-mortar world. You need to go where the greatest number of your ideal customers spend their time.

In lots of ways, putting out videos on different video platforms and services, like YouTube.com, DailyMotion.com, and others, that serve prospects in special niches isn't that different from opening new locations for your brick-and-mortar business, except it doesn't cost as much and requires much less management effort.

Marketing online and marketing offline are not mutually exclusive choices. If you want to use social media strategy to dominate your market, it is important to market where your prospects are, both online as well as offline.

Mistake 21: Emotional Attachments

I just met with a company who knew how to generate a ton of traffic to a special offer on their website.

The traffic to their website was comprised of many of their ideal prospects. The offer seemed valuable enough, and all the site visitors had to do to take advantage of that offer was to enter their name and email address.

Unfortunately, almost nobody took action. The company was devastated, frustrated, and disappointed.

Here's the lesson: It didn't matter if they thought their special offer was a good one, because the marketplace taught them it wasn't.

They also learned the value of having a large tribe of social media followers and solid, targeted Internet traffic to their website so they could find out quickly if their offer would hit or miss.

The special offer designed to capture leads was not a tattoo; they could change it easily and quickly in the hopes of achieving better results.

Here's the point: If a special offer designed to capture leads or orders isn't working, change it quickly and move on. Don't have too much emotional attachment to being right or wrong about what you thought your prospects did or didn't want.

If you ask enough of them, they will tell you. Just listen.

Mistake 22: Failing to Think (and Act) Like a Rock Star

Do you remember what it was like to follow music before the days of music videos? For those of you who grew up after the creation of MTV or don't remember the days when all they did was play music videos, then I challenge you to imagine what it was like for those of us who are a bit older.

Our choices were limited. We could buy a band's record, listen to their songs on the radio, and read about them in magazines. If we were lucky, our favorite band might come play a concert once a year and that was about all we got to see of them.

Videos, podcasts, blogs, social media, and websites changed everything. Today, we get to see band interviews, viral marketing videos, and concert footage by simply logging on to YouTube, other social media services, and even the bands' websites.

YouTube marketing, and video marketing in general, makes it possible for you to promote your business and your brand in your industry niche just like rock stars learned to do in theirs.

Video allows you to give the public intimacy without being intimate. If you aren't willing to make Internet video production, blogging, and status updates at popular social media sites part of your Internet marketing strategy, then it is my belief that you will be forgotten or ignored in the wake of those who do.

Mistake 23: Creating Commercials

How do you feel about commercials you see on TV? Why do you feel that way?

I readily admit that I can't stand commercials. It drives me nuts when stuff gets shoved in my face and interferes with what I want and am trying to do. My dislike for commercials is so strong that I almost never watch live television anymore and record the programs I am interested in using my digital recorder. That way, I can fast-forward through the commercials. Perhaps you can relate.

I had a client who was going to do some YouTube marketing and video marketing. They knew that their best customers almost always went online to do research before making the significant investment required for their services. They created video scripts that answered questions their potential clients frequently asked them. We produced the videos and submitted them for our client's review.

Then it happened. Someone said, "Hey, let's put our music and jingle at the end of it—the owner loves hearing that." I scratched my head, because I knew where the conversation was going. "Let's put our slogan at the end, too," they said.

I had just one question. What does the owner love more, hearing the jingle or getting more customers? They almost ruined a web video campaign by turning it into a lousy commercial.

Look around. There are all kinds of cool services on the Internet that you can get for free if you agree to let them put ads in front of you. Many of those same services will allow you to skip ads or not see them at all if you agree to pay a fee.

Why do you think people are willing to pay NOT to see ads? The answer is they don't like them and don't want them. There is a lesson there.

Why would you invest advertising dollars to interact with potential clients in a manner that they are willing to PAY MONEY to AVOID?

Don't make the mistake of ruining otherwise valuable social media marketing content by turning it into some lame commercial that will only repel the people you want to attract.

Mistake 24: Becoming a One Trick Pony

I had a prospect for my social media marketing consulting services tell me that social media marketing had been a waste of time.

To make a long story short, they only had a few places to showcase their expertise online. They had a website and Facebook page and expected a bunch of their ideal prospects to find them.

Their Internet marketing and online marketing efforts were failing because of two things. They weren't putting out enough new content on a regular basis. And they weren't putting it out in enough places.

Let's pretend you produced a television show or a radio show or had a column in your local newspaper or business journal. Let's also pretend that when your prospects tuned in, they only got to see the same old stuff, week after week. How long do you think people would keep coming back? How often would they tell others to check you out?

Consider this. What if you only had a column in the local newspaper, and that was the only place you had to showcase and share your ideas and business solutions?

The rules of video, online, and social media marketing are very similar to the regular rules of marketing in traditional media channels. You need to be in as many different media channels as possible.

Video sites, podcast sites, social bookmarking sites, blog sites, and status sites should all be part of your online marketing presence. On top of that, you need to put out fresh content regularly and do so for the same reasons you would if you were marketing through traditional media outlets.

Mistake 25: Failing to Answer Objections and Frequently Asked Questions

How are social media marketing, online marketing, video marketing, and email marketing like a weight loss campaign?

If you want to lose weight, everybody knows that you get the best results by eating high-quality, healthy foods in the right portions and exercising regularly, too. It is important to do both.

If you join a gym, hire a personal trainer and a dietician, and don't exercise or eat right, there is only one person to blame. It isn't the trainer, the dietician, or the person who owns the gym. It is your responsibility.

A personal trainer or dietician can guide you down a healthy pathway and help you achieve better results in less time. However, if you don't put in the work that is necessary, you'll fail.

If you don't know what kind of content your ideal prospects would value most, then let me encourage you to start by answering the questions about your products, services, or industry that people ask you about the most. If there are objections or misconceptions regarding your expertise, then providing content that addresses them can also become quite popular.

Mistake 26: Confusing Rank With Authority and Trying to Lead Anyway

I was watching an episode of *Celebrity Apprentice.* For those of you who don't watch it, the premise is that there are two teams of celebrities that are given a task and the team leader of the winning team wins a bunch of money for a charity that is important to him or her.

The losing team has to go into Donald Trump's boardroom, where they discuss what went wrong and then try to determine who is to blame for the loss. Then someone from the losing team is eliminated from the competition.

Both team leaders want to win money for their charity. Neither team leader wants to face elimination.

In this particular episode, the task was to come up with a short jingle and stage performance to promote a particular company's product and service.

Former Miss Universe, Dayana Mendoza, volunteered to lead a team consisting of Lisa Lampanelli, a talented professional comedian, and *American Idol* finalist Clay Aiken.

Dayana was smart, beautiful, and friendly, and she spoke multiple languages. By all accounts, she was and is a very capable and exceptional person.

However, under her leadership, her team lost. When her team performance was dissected by Mr. Trump in the boardroom, things got ugly.

English wasn't her first language and she had no musical experience, and instead of relying on talented and experienced team members who did, she tried to direct a project without a clue about how to do it.

Clay made a comment suggesting that Dayana's team leadership during this project was more like the "blind leading the seeing" and went on to describe how her presence made things take much longer than was necessary.

The lesson I learned watching that episode translates very well into the world of video, social media, and online marketing.

If you are a business owner or an executive in charge of marketing, then my advice to you is to get some social media training; talk to Internet marketing experts and social media consultants with proven track records who can DEMONSTRATE the impact of their strategies and work.

Then my advice is to encourage you NOT to make the same mistake as Dayana. When you get ready to hire a social media agency or online marketing expert, be sure to tell them what you want them to accomplish and let them know what time and resources are available. Don't tell them HOW you want them to do their job.

Why? Because if you knew what you were doing, you wouldn't need them. You may be the boss/customer (you have the rank), but remember that your position doesn't give you the technical knowledge to be the authority and lead the way.

If the social media consultants or Internet marketing strategists are any good, they won't want their name associated with the results of a project directed by the least skilled and least knowledgeable person on the team, regardless of how motivated and well intentioned you may be. They know it won't produce the kind of results they can use to showcase their skills and drive up the price for their services.

You may not be starring on *Celebrity Apprentice*. You may not have to justify your decisions in front of Mr. Trump. However, if you fail to heed my advice, you might find yourself knee-deep in the middle of an expensive and time-consuming project only to be told by the frustrated experts on the team of people you hired to help you that "You're fired."

Mistake 27: Trying to Understand Everything Before Doing Anything

When you dive into video, online, and social media marketing, you'll soon discover how easy it is to get overwhelmed by technical details and minutia. If you're not careful, you'll end up wasting time and money unnecessarily.

Think about this. When you need to go somewhere, you know you can get in a car, turn a key, look through the windshield, turn the steering wheel, and step on the gas to go wherever you want to go.

You may WANT to know all about engines, electricity, oil, spark plugs, and how they all work together, but do you really NEED to in order to drive wherever you want?

Be careful to identify and separate the "want to know" knowledge from the "need to know" knowledge. If you don't, then the consequences can be very time-consuming, expensive, frustrating, and counterproductive.

Mistake 28: Failure to Realize That Text Is Good; Pictures Are Better; Videos Are the Best

Think about the power of a good picture. What's that old saying? A picture is worth a thousand words.

Here's my question. If a picture is worth a thousand words, what is a video worth?

Videos, particularly on YouTube, since Google owns it, are more heavily weighted in search results compared to text. They can also help the video producer tell a more complete story in less time in ways that are more engaging and memorable.

Mistake 29: Blending In

I live just outside the suburbs of St. Louis, Missouri. The other day I decided to take a different route into the city and back. I wanted a change of pace. I easily drove over 150 miles round-trip that day, and here's what I realized when I got home.

I couldn't count the number of billboards I passed alongside of the road. Do you know what else I couldn't do? I couldn't tell you what one of them said. I couldn't tell you about one product or service shown. I couldn't tell you one of the phone numbers or addresses on any of them.

Do you know what I CAN tell you about? I can tell you about the videos that I watched yesterday on Facebook and YouTube that my friends liked. I can tell you about web videos that I watched weeks ago, months ago, and sometimes years ago.

I can also tell you about plenty of YouTube videos I watched over the last year that taught me how to do things I didn't know how to do, regardless of whether or not a friend recommended them.

Mistake 30: Resistance to Change

According to something I read recently on YouTube, "98 of Ad Age's Top 100 advertisers have run campaigns on YouTube and the Google Display Network."

What do you think that means?

Here's what I think it means.

Some of the big boys are finally getting it.

Here's my question. Have you?

I can't emphasize enough how valuable I believe YouTube marketing, and video marketing in general, is to your success online.

Web video lets you tell your story. You can demonstrate how you solve problems. You can let people get to know you, your personality, and your company's culture. You can let them see your products or services in action.

Or you can let them read one of your brochures. Which do you think your ideal prospects would prefer?

Mistake 31: Running From Problems

Business owners everywhere dream of the viral marketing power of web videos.

Here's a warning: If you or your employees screw something up and you don't make it right, then that same power can be used against you. Your dreams of viral marketing opportunities can become a nightmare. Just ask United Airlines.

Go to YouTube and type in "United Breaks Guitars" and see what happens. United Airlines now knows the power of viral marketing, and so do millions of people who watched that video.

Accept responsibility. Do what is right. Take care of your customers. Fix mistakes and do it quickly.

Mistake 32: Trying to Hide Mistakes

Thanks to social media marketing and social media tools, customers have plenty of places to file their complaints. They don't have to fill out a form or wait in a line anymore for a manager to tell them "tough luck" when they have had a bad experience. And they don't have to take no for an answer.

Angry customers can go online and tell everyone. And it's not like the company that is being badmouthed, regardless of whether or not it is deserved, has the power to erase it.

If you own a company and an angry past customer is making it their life's mission to make an example out of you, then use the Internet to turn that past mistake into an opportunity!

Some people might disagree, but I think you should help an angry customer trying to point out a mistake and do it publicly. Demonstrate transparently how your company solves problems and helps customers in need of assistance.

Everyone makes mistakes, and the public realizes it, too. Demonstrate your flexibility and spirit of cooperation in a way that lets the public see your side of the story and your willingness to make things right.

If your angry customer continues to persist after all reasonable public attempts to satisfy them have been exhausted, then public opinion and sympathy may shift from the angry individual to favor your company instead. Your company can showcase the proper way to handle a difficult customer and do what is right.

The public can see authentic, genuine attempts to provide exceptional service and fix mistakes. They appreciate it.

Mistake 33: No Special Offer

Imagine that you are a wide receiver and you are trying out for a job as a professional athlete in the NFL. Your living depends on your ability to outperform almost every athlete in the world in your position. You aren't just playing for fun anymore; this is about business.

You've got lots of things going for you. Let's imagine that you have lightning-fast speed and can run a 40-yard dash in 4 seconds flat. Let's pretend you are 6 foot 8 inches tall and weigh 245 pounds and your body fat percentage is less than 7%. You have a vertical leap of over 40 inches and know how to run receiving routes better than anyone.

Let's pretend that you're big, strong, fast, flexible, smart, and every quarterback's dream, except for one thing. You can't catch a football. You drop every pass.

Unfortunately, companies drop the ball when they forget or fail to include compelling special offers and calls to action at some point during their Internet marketing process that can turn Internet browsers into customers online.

Don't make the same mistake.

Mistake 34: No Free Samples and/or Interaction

I went to the mall today in St. Louis with my son Clayton and was reminded of an offline marketing strategy that successful social media strategists, top social media consultants, and Internet marketing trainers have been trying to drill into the minds of their clients since they started their businesses.

After stopping by his favorite stores, the Apple store, GameStop, and Brookstone, Clayton started to get hungry. I guess it was a lot of work trying to negotiate money out of my wallet for the things he wanted and he needed to refuel.

As we entered the food court, there were 12 different restaurants to choose from. Some had lines of people waiting to buy food and others didn't.

I asked Clayton what he was in the mood for and he said he didn't know. So we decided to walk around and take a look at each of the menus and make a choice.

Six of the 12 restaurants had someone out front offering samples. They held out their hands to offer us a sample and told us what it was. They were also quick to point in the direction of their cash register and tell us the special price.

What happened after we made it around the entire food court? It was time to make a decision, and the only restaurants that either of us considered were ones we had sampled. We both went with the teriyaki chicken and rice from the same restaurant.

While we were sitting at our table eating, I couldn't help but notice the lines in front of the restaurants that were interacting with potential customers and offering free samples. I noticed that with the exception of Chick-fil-A, the lines in front of the restaurants NOT offering samples were almost nonexistent.

What is the lesson from this story? Make sure you include a way to interact with prospects that familiarizes them with your offering, eliminates confusion and minimizes perceived risks of purchasing from you.

Mistake 35: Letting a Hot Lead Get Cold

I signed up to run in a 100-mile ultra-marathon last year. I had never run over 50 miles at once and knew this would be a test of my physical limits.

During a training run with two of my friends who had both completed races of that distance, I asked them about blisters and how to avoid them. They both said I needed to get a book called *Fixing Your Feet* by John Vonhof.

When I was in Barnes and Noble at the mall, I thought I would pick it up and support a brick-and-mortar store. Unfortunately, they didn't have it. They asked me if I wanted to order it. I politely declined and left the store disappointed.

John Vonhof will make money when I buy his book because I trust the advice of my friends who are experienced ultra-marathoners. I also trust the advice of experienced people I meet online in topical discussion forums when they demonstrate specific knowledge and experience that I don't have.

First, word of mouth is still king regardless of whether it takes place during a run with friends, online at a discussion forum, or on some social media or video site like YouTube.

Second, I'd be more inclined to buy books online next time and save myself the trip. Why? Because I left frustrated and disappointed.

The store offered me no incentive to do business with them. If they had one, they didn't tell me what it was. Great Internet marketing companies like Amazon.com almost always have special offers and/or alternative recommendations. Barnes and Noble let me get away.

Regardless of whether you are implementing online marketing strategies or offline marketing strategies, it is imperative that you have some sort of offer, call to action, or alternative recommendation that makes it worth your prospects' time to buy something from you now, especially since they are already willing to make a purchase.

Mistake 36: Failure to Appeal to Those Who Want to Work and Play

My wife Melissa is always trying to get my son Clayton to read. We both think TV in moderation is OK, but we would much rather have our son using his brain and learning something of value.

She was teaching a yoga class nearby and dropped Clayton and me off at the mall in St. Louis. We visited all the usual stores, like the Apple Store, the sporting goods store, and, of course, GameStop. We also went into Barnes and Noble.

On the drive home, Melissa asked Clayton if he saw any books he wanted or liked. She was disappointed when she found out he didn't buy any and spent most of his time in the section of the store showing videos.

Here's what I found interesting. In a huge store full of books, he spent his time almost exclusively in the dinky little section containing a minimal selection of movies and videos.

When surrounded by an almost unlimited number of options of things to read, he was most interested in a tiny selection of movies and videos. Is there a lesson here?

I think so. People love to watch TV and videos. They associate it with fun, excitement, and entertainment. When I talk to my son about books and reading, he associates it with schoolwork.

When preparing your marketing content, you don't have to choose between delivering your message using text, audio, or video. You can, and should, do it all.

Mistake 37: Worrying About What Others Are Doing

When I was 7 years old, my parents signed me up to run AAU track, and one of the earliest pieces of advice that I can recall from over 30 years ago still applies today in the world of Internet and video marketing.

What was that advice? Whenever you're racing, don't ever look back. My coaches always told me to run my best race and give everything I had every time I stepped onto the starting line.

If I looked back, then all kinds of bad things could happen. I could break my stride and lose a fraction of a second that could change the outcome of a race. If my competitor saw me look back, they might be encouraged to dig deeper and go harder than they might have if they thought I felt strong and wasn't about to crack. If I looked back and saw that I had it in the bag, the temptation to back off my pace could creep up, too.

When it comes to online and video marketing, the coaching advice I have for you is the same as the advice that my AAU track coaches gave me when I was first starting to enter competitive sports.

When you distribute your marketing content online, always put your best foot forward and work on making your best better. Focus your attention on sharing ideas and strategies that your ideal customers will value most, and don't dilute that focus to worry about what your competitors are or aren't doing.

Let them worry about you. Let them trip. Let them ease up when they should be pushing. When you catch them looking back, commenting on your ideas or half-heartedly trying to duplicate them, you will know you are doing it right.

Mistake 38: Bringing the Boredom

Did you know that I could give you the best strategies in the world related to video, social media, and online marketing and you would still be likely to fail if you didn't watch out for one HUGE mistake that SHOULD be obvious but often isn't?

It's remarkably simple. Ad agencies and consultants might be reluctant to tell you what I'm about to say because they have a fear of getting fired. Nobody likes to be the messenger who gets shot for delivering bad news.

I'm willing to risk it. So I'll say it. Nobody wants to read, watch, or listen to drivel about boring products or services, nor are they likely to share it either. If you have viral marketing aspirations for your online marketing campaigns and you aren't inspiring, entertaining, or solving problems for your ideal prospects, forget it. You are wasting your time.

Mistake 39: Chasing the "Next Big Thing"

People are always asking me what I think is the next big thing when it comes to online, video, and social media marketing sites. The questions are almost always asked the same way. People will often come up to me after reading some random blog or article and say something like "I heard that I should learn how to market on _____ (insert newest social media site name here). It seems like everybody is doing it."

Instead of chasing the "next big thing," my advice to you is to focus on your overall content strategy and integrate the social media and online marketing tools that best support it on the sites that draw the affection of your ideal prospects.

Automation and advanced strategies developed for the "current big thing" that strategically support the distribution of your content may deliver far more consistent and reliable results than you are likely to get from the next big thing.

Additionally, when your focus is on content creation and you create it using all sorts of formats (videos, podcasts, articles, etc.), then you will always have material ready for whichever sites rise in popularity even when others start to fall.

Social networks will come and go. The need for quality content will always remain, regardless of which social networks it's delivered through.

Mistake 40: Failing to Focus on the Fundamentals

I used to love watching ESPN when I was a kid. I loved sports and still do. Now, as a parent, I can see why my parents weren't such big fans.

When I was out on the driveway as a kid with my basketball and my dad, he wanted to work on fundamentals like bounce passes and layups. I wanted to dribble around my back and, through my legs and jack up 3-point shots every time I got the chance.

I saw all the flashy highlights on ESPN and wanted to do the same. Dad knew I needed the fundamentals first, and he had the patience of a saint.

When it comes to video, social media, and online marketing, what are the fundamentals?

The answer is simple. It is keyword research.

Until you know the traffic, competition, relevance, and commercial intent associated with the words and phrases you plan to make the cornerstone of your online marketing efforts, social media posts, and video scripts, you probably aren't ready for the fancy stuff.

Mistake 41: Failing to Give People What They Want ... First

People have been asking me what I think are the best ways to respond to the changes in Google.

Google is getting smarter. It has amazing information about the users of all its different services, and it is connecting the dots to better determine what people really want to know, faster. What people really want to know is not necessarily what they've typically typed into search engines in the past.

Google and YouTube can tell how long people watch your videos and how much time they spend on your site. They also know what people typed in the search engines to get to your content in the first place.

Short visits suggest that the content wasn't as relevant to the person doing the search as it could have been. What does that mean to you as part of your content development strategy?

The answer is simple. Quit trying to push your stuff down people's throats. Answer their questions first. Solve their problems first. Give them what they were looking for first. Do it fast.

If prospects want answers to questions or solutions to their problems, then don't beat around the bush or start rattling off about your company, how long you've been in business, your great selection, your cheap prices, and all kinds of other stuff they don't care about or won't believe anyway.

Also, it is becoming more important to consider the intentions of people performing searches on the Internet. Why? Because Google is already doing it.

Align the creation of your content and your strategies for distribution of that content in ways that give searchers what they really want to find, even if it isn't what they typed into the search bar.

With Google's "Hummingbird" algorithm update, we noticed stark differences in the results that were delivered for similar searches when compared to Bing or Yahoo, which as of the date of this writing are still relatively dependent on keywords. Why? Google never gives away its secrets, but Rand Fishkin (see http://www.MOZ.com) suggests it has to do with what he calls "co-occurrence." Simplified, it means that Google can look across the Internet and make evaluations about what is and isn't related and relevant INDEPENDENT OF and IN ADDITION TO the words and phrases appearing on a site.

If you fail, Google will know and it will hurt your business online. If you succeed, Google will know and it will help.

Mistake 42: Writing Scripts for Search Engines Instead of People

People have been asking me about how they should write their content for the highest rankings in Google and the other key search engines.

The answer may be simpler than you think. Create content for human beings first, and the search engines later.

In other words, answer people's questions and solve their problems as if they were standing in front of you having a conversation. Then find out ways to go back and include keyword phrases that people are searching for online.

When you keep those two priorities in order, then you are more likely to get your content found in search engines and shared throughout social media channels than ignored or ridiculed.

Mistake 43: Forfeit and Non-participation

Are you a skeptic when it comes to using social media for business? Do you question the effectiveness and ROI of all the video, social media, and online marketing strategies you read about?

You should. I live in St. Louis, and Missouri is affectionately known as the "Show-Me State" for good reason. People around here want to see proof.

A bit of skepticism is healthy. However, too much of a "wait and see attitude" can put you so far behind that you might not ever catch up. Or if you do, it could take far longer to secure a profitable online presence and cost much more than was necessary.

If you're like most savvy business owners, you want guarantees that your efforts will pay off. Here's one thing I can guarantee: If people can't find you and don't know you exist, it's like losing your business opportunities by forfeit. If you don't play, it is impossible to win.

Mistake 44: Failing to Market Globally Even If Your Prospects Are Local

If you're a local business owner who sells products or services locally, you might not think it would be worth your time to utilize things like video marketing, social media, or online marketing outside of your local market area.

What if I told you that you could be wrong? Here's my explanation.

I had a client, who was a doctor in St. Louis, get a call from a person located in the country of Ecuador. Evidently, the parent in Ecuador had a child attending St. Louis University who needed a specialized form of treatment. The parent learned about the treatment and my client from watching YouTube marketing videos.

Another client got a home repair project because a local St. Louis lady asked her brother in New York to find a St. Louis contractor he trusted, and my client told me this story and explained how the brother watched my client's YouTube videos and told the sister to call him.

Advertising agents at advertising agencies and advertising firms always tell you to target your market because it costs so much to advertise. It's too expensive to be wasteful.

However, when it comes to YouTube marketing and video marketing, it doesn't cost any more for someone in your area to see your web videos than it does for someone halfway around the world.

Mistake 45: Failure to Reap the Rewards of Failed Ad Campaigns

Advertising firms like to promise you exposure for your business as a result of their advertising. They like to claim advertising is a good investment, even when it isn't generating new clients.

They could be right, but not for the reasons you may be thinking. If you aren't getting new clients when you advertise, you are still getting something of value.

What you are getting is feedback. It is valuable because it is telling you that you need to change your message or change your approach. You might need to change both.

If you are trying to advertise on TV or radio or in a newspaper, it means you are trying to take people's attention away from something else they value and get them to pay attention to what you want them to know or remember about your product or service. It's an interruption, and just because so many other vendors interrupt them with ads, it doesn't mean you should, too.

If your product or service solves common problems, then it might be a better idea to consider changing your approach. It might be more effective to create a YouTube video, podcast, or article that helps them. Content marketing leveraged through popular social media services like Facebook and Twitter creates new avenues for people to find out about you and your services without being interrupted.

If your marketing content still falls flat and fails to generate more business regardless of the channels and forms it is delivered in, then perhaps you should be thankful that you have discovered a message that isn't working. Take it as feedback that you need to change it. When looking for ways to grow your business, I encourage you to regard flexibility and feedback as two of your greatest assets.

Mistake 46: Ignoring Your Ratings

Have you ever wondered why TV shows get canceled even when you like them? The answer is a simple one. There weren't enough other people who liked the show to build a significant audience. The content wasn't powerful enough to generate conversations and buzz.

I want to challenge you to think of producing your marketing content as if you were a TV producer, and even more so if you are into YouTube marketing and video marketing. TV producers don't keep remaking shows that aren't pulling an audience, and neither should you. If you aren't building an audience and people aren't sharing your content with others, then you can use that feedback to change your approach.

TV producers create all kinds of shows, and when they get a hit, people can't stop talking about it. The audience builds a bigger audience.

When you put out content about how your products or services help people in a way that connects with your ideal audience, then they will want to share it, too, with a lot more people.

The rewards of viral marketing are possible, but only when the content is worthy. I encourage you to pay attention to the feedback you get, not as a fan who wants the content, but as a producer who wants an excited and growing audience.

Mistake 47: Failure to Make Heroes Out of Influencers

Besides the obvious importance of providing content that others find amusing, inspiring, or informative, there is one other thing to consider that might be the deal clincher. It will require you to think differently than you might have been taught by a local advertising firm or advertising agent who is simply trying to help you get noticed and/or remembered.

I challenge you to create content that other people want to share. For example, if you want to reach business owners, put out content that accountants would want to share with their clients (who also happen to be your best prospects). It makes the accountant look proactive, caring, and helpful while getting you additional exposure from a position of subject matter authority.

For example, I have a friend who is a conservative and is also African American. When he puts out content, highly motivated, politically active conservatives spread it like wildfire throughout all their social media channels. Why? Because when he produces content that expresses their similar viewpoints, they can share those ideas with people everywhere without being unfairly characterized as racists, especially since race has nothing to do with their viewpoints.

The bottom line is that I encourage you to create content that other people benefit from when they share it with the people in their sphere of influence. Put out content that lawyers can share with their clients, accountants can share with theirs, and consultants and authors can share with theirs, and the chances of good things coming your way will go up significantly.

Mistake 48: Failure to Recognize the Market Value of Your Online Real Estate

If I buy a radio ad, it plays and goes away. If I buy a newspaper ad, it gets crumpled up and thrown away. There's nothing that really lasts, unless I keep spending money to put new ads up to replace the old ones.

In the advertising world, if you've got a ton of money, then you can be a bully in your market. It doesn't necessarily work that way when it comes to space online.

One thing that most business owners who haven't used social media for business don't recognize is the asset they can create by occupying and dominating online space in their niche. It's like REALLY valuable real estate, and there is only so much of the really good stuff in your niche.

As a small business, one of your goals should be to lock down the top spaces in search engines related to the most profitable keywords. If you do this successfully, you may end up getting bought out by one of the biggest companies in your industry.

Here's the kicker. You may get a ridiculous offer, but not because of the value of your company, products, or sales or the skills of their management team. It may not even be because of your brand or name recognition.

It could simply come down to one thing. The industry leaders (or the up-and-coming companies who want to be the industry leaders) have been beaten to the punch and don't have the time, money, or expertise to displace the small business that knew how to dominate and gobble up the most profitable online space related to their products and services.

The big players can't afford to keep losing big opportunities. They can't afford to keep getting ignored online. The size of their budgets doesn't guarantee their success over the "little guy," especially when the "little guy" knows how to market online. It's easier for the big players to write a big check, buy the company, and keep all the leads for themselves.

Mistake 49: Forgetting the Relationship Between Offline Service and Online Sales

Want to know what you and your business can do offline that can make or break your sales revenue online? It's really easy. Anyone can do it.

Let me give you a real-life example. I live in St. Louis, Missouri, and I wanted a sports car. To be specific, I wanted a Porsche Boxster convertible. I went to Cars.com and did a search for all the Porsche Boxsters available for sale within a 500-mile radius. I compared prices and checked CarFax reports for several months.

One day, I found exactly what I was looking for. It was a metallic grey car with black leather interior, and it only had 28,000 miles. It was located in Des Moines, Iowa, at Stew Hansen Hyundai. It was a dealership with upfront pricing and they had it priced to sell.

I called up the sales rep, Bryan, and asked him all sorts of questions. By the time we were finished, I had put down a deposit and made plans to go to Des Moines and check it out on the contingency that it was everything he described and that I would get a warranty so I wouldn't get stuck in the middle of nowhere if it broke down on the way home.

His sales manager, Danny, agreed and gave me a 1-month, 1,000-mile warranty on the drive train and anything they inspected. I went online and read reviews of their dealership. I read comments about my sales rep, too. They were all positive. The CarFax reports were solid, too. I felt comfortable.

When I got home with the car, it looked like there might be a problem that wasn't on the drive train or on the list of things they inspected.

I spoke with the Danny, the sales manager. He could have insisted that I drive the vehicle back to their location to examine and/or service it. He could have told me tough luck.

And if he did, then I wouldn't be singing the praises of this dealership or their management team all over the Internet. In fact, it could have very easily been the opposite.

He asked me to go to a Porsche dealership here in St. Louis and have it evaluated and let him know what the bill was. He offered to work with me to defray costs even though he "technically" didn't have to. In the end, it turned out to be nothing, but they were ready to stand behind it and that was what made me such a fan.

Here's what my sales rep, Bryan, the sales manager, Danny, and the rest of the dealership at Stew Hansen Hyundai understand that many others don't. Outstanding customer service OFFLINE can be the best ONLINE sales strategy you can have.

Why? They could have hired the best advertising agencies in the country to create the coolest ads ever and it wouldn't have mattered to me one bit. They could have hired social media strategists, but there was nothing they could have done to stop angry customers from damaging their reputation online.

They could, however, make sure they kept customers from becoming angry. They could choose to do the little "extras" that make customers happy and want to tell others online. And that's exactly what they did.

Word of mouth travels quickly. Words on keyboards do, too, and because they are on the Internet and don't get erased easily, if ever, it is critical that you think of the consequences of your words and actions with your customers.

Mistake 50: Creating Content That Won't Get Discovered or Engage Ideal Prospects

Want a simple little tip that can help your content get found by more of your ideal prospects and engage them quickly?

Assuming you have done your keyword research, it then becomes important for you to make sure those keywords are actually included in the content you produce online.

If you're doing article marketing, Facebook marketing, YouTube marketing, and video marketing, it is important to include your keywords.

Here's a simple way to get about five of them in one sentence AND capture the attention of your ideal prospects. Simply ask them if they are looking for X, Y, and Z and trying to avoid A and B.

You accomplish two things in one sentence. First, you increase your chances of getting found by someone who is entering those keywords in their searches online. Second, you engage an ideal prospect quickly if they find your question enticing.

Mistake 51: Failure to Position as a Better Alternative

Want a simple online marketing strategy and tip that can help you position yourself and your content as an alternative to popular online searches for things offered by your competitors? It's kind of like a bait-and-switch strategy ... except that it is good and ethical, too.

People aren't interested in your product. They are interested in what your product does for them. You may offer an alternative means to solving a common problem. However, if few people know about it, then they aren't looking for it in large numbers online.

Here's something you CAN do about it. Explain that you AREN'T X, Y, or Z, but that you solve the same problems in a different way that is better because of A, B, and C. Make sure that whatever you put in your content to represent X, Y, and Z are good keywords and keyword phrases that lots of your ideal prospects are actively searching for.

If you're doing article marketing, Facebook marketing, YouTube marketing, or other types of video marketing, it is very important to include the right keywords. Sometimes the best keywords have more to do with your competitors than they do you or your company.

Mistake 52: Failing to Create Content That Features Your Competition

Want your content to get found when people are looking for your product OR your competitors?

If you know how to do this, you can get found when people do online searches for their products as well as yours!

This tip may help increase your chances for success. Create comparison content.

Again, if you're doing article marketing, Facebook marketing, YouTube marketing, or other types of video marketing, it is VERY important to include the right keywords. Make sure you include your competitor's product or name against your own in the title, content, tags, and descriptions of any content you distribute online.

Mistake 53: Failing to Work With the Willing

My friend Tom Ruwitch (see http://www.MarketVolt.com) was talking to a group of business owners in St. Louis recently. He is an expert in email marketing and runs a company called MarketVolt.

He said that one of the biggest direct marketing mistakes businesspeople make is not wanting to be a pest, so they don't send anything out. I agree with him and see it, too.

His solution was a simple one. He told the entrepreneurs in the group to separate prospects from suspects by tracking who opens and responds to follow-up emails and contacts.

Are you working with the willing once they have been identified and separated? Or is your shotgun approach to direct marketing positioning you as a pest with the wrong people?

Mistake 54: Failure to Create Evangelists

The online marketing, search engine optimization (SEO), and social media marketing world is always buzzing whenever Google makes changes to its algorithms. When the strategies that used to help now cause harm to online rankings, it leaves people scrambling and wondering what to do next.

Google wants natural links, not the kind of artificial, "manufactured" links that SEO professionals have made their living creating for people, until recently.

Who do you hire to do that? How do you manage them? How do you know if they are doing a good job?

The answer is you don't.

If you know the secret I'm getting ready to tell you, then you can get all kinds of natural links and social media buzz for free. The best part is that they are what Google has been wanting all along.

After I completed the ultra-marathon and posted some pictures on Facebook, one of my fraternity brothers responded and told me he was getting ready to run his first 50-mile race a few weeks later.

Since it was going to be his first, I knew that his nutrition plan (or lack thereof) might make or break his race and might even be more important than his physical training. So I posted a link on his Facebook wall to an amazing resource that NO extreme endurance athlete should be without.

What was it? I posted a link to a pdf document put out by Hammer Nutrition called "The Endurance Athlete's Guide to Success," and it contained over 100 pages of rock-solid fueling and hydration advice from some of the world's leading authorities. It is a MUST READ. It's THAT unique, and people can't get that kind of information just anywhere. The ideas and information I've gotten from that guide have served me well, and I knew I was doing him a favor by sharing it with him. I wanted to help and felt good that I could.

Who wins? Hammer Nutrition wins because I tell anyone I meet who is contemplating an extreme event about their knowledge base and products. I win because I did something nice for a friend who appreciates it. My friend wins because he might finish a race he otherwise might not have completed. He is bound to finish it faster and suffer less.

I can't tell you how many people are now customers of Hammer Nutrition because of my referrals. I refer them because they don't sell food. They teach people how to fuel their body in extreme conditions and accomplish their goals.

Guess what? There are lots of people just like me who do the same thing. We spread the gospel. We are evangelists for things we believe will help others. We create natural, real, authentic links and conversations all over the Internet and social media sites without getting paid by the companies we promote.

If you want evangelists for your company, products, or services, then all you need to do is put out amazing content that helps people. If it is really good, then people will feel good about sharing it with others and everybody wins.

You don't need advertising firms, advertising agencies, or advertising agents to write slick ads. You need great content.

You don't need social media consultants, social media training companies, or social media strategists to micromanage your posts either.

Put out AMAZING, UNIQUE, and VALUABLE content that helps others and they will help you, too.

Mistake 55: Playing It Too Safe

Want someone to make a ridiculously big offer to buy your company? What if I told you about a way that has very little to do with the quality of your products, services, location, experience, years of experience, or customer list? What if I told you it has very little to do with your building, your equipment, or other assets except one? What if I told you that you could make the industry giants open their checkbooks up to you even if you are just a one-man or one-woman shop?

Would you want to know how?

As more and more prospects go online to research products and services they want to buy and fewer people rely on traditional lead sources like the Yellow Pages, you can become a real threat to the big companies' empires if you lock up the virtual real estate around the most valuable keyword phrases in your industry.

While the big boys sit around their conference rooms, dabbling in social media marketing and trying to play it safe, you could be monopolizing the online lead sources of the future. If you can do that well, at some point in time they are likely to realize that it will be easier, faster, and cheaper to write you a big check than it will be to displace your fortified positions all across the Internet.

Mistake 56: Unnecessarily Using Pushy Salespeople

Here's a question for you: Why do companies hire pushy high-pressure salespeople? I guess that there are still some who argue that it works, at least in the short term, especially if they work for a company that has no regard for a business relationship, the lifetime value of a customer, or their reputation.

Because of the Internet, product knowledge has never been easier to acquire. In my opinion, companies who fail to embrace web videos as a virtual form of a salesperson are limiting their sales potential by ignoring the will of a large segment of potential customers who would rather not have to interact with a salesperson at all regardless of whether or not they are pushy.

Not all prospects are extroverts. Some would rather be left alone to research and buy online. Virtual salespeople can provide solutions and answers without all the pressure and enhance the customer experience and maximize the probability of repeat orders and referrals.

Mistake 57: Failure to Diversify Your Online Lead Sources

Have you ever heard the saying, "Don't put all your eggs in one basket?" When it comes to social media marketing, online marketing, video marketing, YouTube marketing, and Facebook marketing, that advice still holds true.

When Google changed its algorithms, lots of businesses that relied almost exclusively on leads from high Google rankings found themselves in DEEP trouble, fast. The best social media strategists will all tell you that it is critical to generate leads from a wide variety of unrelated online sources.

If you aren't making videos, creating articles, distributing blog posts, and updating content on status sites like Twitter or Facebook, then you might want to start. Diversify your risks and maximize your opportunity.

Mistake 58: Trying to Catch Fish in Empty Ponds

Who is your ideal customer, and where do they go for information? That's a question Dale Furtwengler, author of the book *Pricing for Profit* (see http://www.PricingForProfitBook.com), asked an audience he was speaking to recently.

He is also a consultant who practices what he preaches. He asked a focus group of his ideal customers how they made the decision to hire consultants. They told him that they needed to hear a consultant speak, read their articles, or have one recommended by people they trusted. Nothing else mattered.

Advertising agents would have been wasting their time trying to sell Dale advertising services, because Dale knew it wouldn't work with his target audience. Why? Because they told him so.

Mistake 59: Not Marketing to the Maybes

My friend Tom Ruwitch, who is the president of the email marketing company MarketVolt in St. Louis (see http://www.marketvolt.com), made a comment I wanted to share with you.

Tom said, "A sales pitch only creates value for someone who is already a buyer." But what about the vast majority of people who aren't ready to buy yet? Are you "marketing to the maybes," as Tom calls it?

Would you rather focus your marketing efforts on the 1% or 2% of people who are ready to buy now or the rest of them who will buy eventually if you reach out and continually engage them?

The answer is both. They aren't mutually exclusive choices.

Mistake 60: Being Too Slick /Lacking Authenticity

When it comes to video marketing on YouTube and other video sites, I don't always believe it is necessary to edit every little mistake. If you're shooting a video and you fumble or stumble on a word, in many cases I would tell you not to sweat it.

So what if you're not perfect? Nobody is. It's OK to be human. People like authenticity. Don't be surprised if some of your YouTube marketing efforts actually relate better to your ideal prospects if you show your vulnerabilities once in a while.

I'm not saying you should allow a bunch of major screwups, but it's OK if you aren't perfect. In lots of cases, it's OK if you don't sweat the small stuff.

Additionally, I've seen people who were so obsessed with the idea of perfection that almost nothing they did was good enough to "go public" and they failed to serve the needs of their markets who were craving their knowledge. They chose to serve their egos instead of the prospects who needed their help most.

Mistake 61: Forgetting That a Little Customer Can Have a Big Voice

I want to share a story so you don't make the same mistake.

I own a bicycle made by a bicycle company we will call "XYZ." One of the reasons I bought that bicycle was because of the lifetime warranty on the frame. I was told by the owner of the bicycle shop where I bought it that as long as I didn't crash it, if I got any cracks on my frame it would be replaced.

The bike shop was reputable. "XYZ" is a reputable company. For those reasons, I felt comfortable buying an expensive bike.

The other day I was messing around on Facebook. One of my friends who is a local mountain bike racer posted a picture of his bike and claimed that he had a crack in the frame that "XYZ" refused to acknowledge. Evidently, he had multiple discussions with their customer service team and got no satisfaction from them.

Since then, he has posted on his Facebook page that he wants to make it his "second job" to tell everybody he can about the poor customer service and treatment that he received from "XYZ." He has placed stickers on his bicycle that in not-so-nice terms say "F*** XYZ."

The cyclists in his peer group are "XYZ's" ideal target market. "XYZ" spends lots of money trying to gain influence and maintain credibility within this cycling community.

My friend's bike and the comments that he has stickered onto it can't be ignored. As you can imagine, the other racers see his bike and ask him what happened. He is more than happy to tell his story.

Between his comments on Facebook and his conversation-starting stickers on his bike, he can undo images, branding, and credibility that have cost "XYZ" countless dollars and years of effort.

He is continuing to race his mountain bike and has pledged that if his bike breaks and he gets hurt, he will be sure to sue "XYZ" because of it.

"XYZ" may have won the battle. But by denying his claim and refusing to honor their warranty, they are likely to lose the war.

This one unsatisfied customer can prevent all kinds of other people from becoming "XYZ" customers. It's his mission.

When information gets circulated on the Internet, it's not like "XYZ" can just go out and erase it. In fact, it's more like the opposite. When he shows up at races all over the country, "XYZ" can't make him go away.

If you mistreat a customer, they won't just go away. They may decide to tell anyone and everyone who will listen. Thanks to social media and the Internet, the "little guy" can have a big voice!

Mistake 62: Giving Up Too Soon

If you are 300 pounds overweight, eat as much as three grown adults on any given day, and don't exercise, and you don't want to change your diet or work out, it is not realistic to expect drastic improvements in your health and wellness. Wouldn't it be nice if there was a magic pill that existed that could allow you to eat as much as you want of whatever you want without ever having to exercise? Well, as far as I know, it doesn't exist yet.

How would you like to dramatically increase the number of hits on your business's website? How would you like to increase the quality of the prospects who visit your site? How would you like to convert more prospects into customers without lifting a finger? How would you like to be able to dramatically improve your results online without spending any money? How would you like to dominate the search engines for your keyword phrases immediately?

I hate to break it to you, but when it comes to online marketing results, there's no magic pill that will give you all of those things either. If you find somebody offering you all of those things, grab your wallet or purse and run.

What I believe is most important is that you're willing to do whatever it takes, for as long as it takes. It's important that you notice what online marketing and social media strategies are working and keep adjusting your approach until you get what you're after.

In one of my first jobs out of college, I worked for a man named Paul Cummings, and he once told me, "The road to the top goes straight through the dump."

He told me that if I didn't think I could stand the stench, I shouldn't start the trip. His advice still rings true when it comes to online marketing. There are no shortcuts. There are no magic wands.

There are reliable strategies. There are reliable tactics. If they are applied correctly, then the desired results are likely to occur if you give them enough time to work.

Be patient. Be diligent. Do not give up until you get the results you are seeking. Or don't start the trip.

Mistake 63: Advertising for Your Competitors

I believe that video production and distribution is the cornerstone of many successful online marketing campaigns.

When you begin creating new content on your online video channels, some services may ask if you wish to allow advertisements on your videos. What do you think you should do? Should you allow advertising? Or should you say no?

If you are promoting a solution to a problem, it might not make sense to allow advertisements from competitors to show up on your videos. The last thing you may want to do is produce web videos that attract your ideal prospects and then show them offers from your competitors.

If you are only creating content that will be of value to your ideal market, but you are not promoting a solution that is a product or service offered by your company, and you would like to share in revenue that the video hosting site generates by selling advertising on your videos, then advertising may not be a bad idea.

However, you need to choose what is most important. Is it more important to earn a little bit of revenue from advertising? Or is it more important to promote solutions to problems that are solved by your company's products or services and get paid for those instead? It all comes down to what's most important.

Mistake 64: Doing What Everyone Else Is Doing

I'm a huge fan of Tim Ferris's book *The 4-Hour Workweek*. In that book, he says that if what you're doing isn't working, try the opposite. I respect his contrarian views.

In fact, there may be a way that those same views can help you build your business. If you are engaged in social media marketing, video marketing, and other online marketing strategies, then you know how important it is to be able to capture and maintain the attention of your ideal prospects for as long as you possibly can. Want to know where you can get some fresh ideas?

I was staying in a hotel in Chattanooga, Tennessee, recently and I couldn't sleep. I was scrolling through the television channels and saw a bunch of infomercials.

Most of them were boring and they all sounded the same, except one. While most infomercials were bragging about how great their products or services were and showing testimonials, there was one that did the opposite.

It had some guy promoting a book or a book series about how to get free money. The interesting thing was the way he set it up.

He positioned his infomercial as if it was an investigative report trying to expose a scam.

Instead of making an outrageous claim and letting the viewer doubt it, he did the opposite. He had an actress posing as an investigative reporter treating the claims as if they may not be true and then going to visit with the people who made these claims and asking them for proof.

It was an interesting change of pace. Why? Because the actress posing as a reporter was basically questioning his credibility, calling his claims potential scams and demanding proof as if she didn't believe them.

Nobody wants to get ripped off. Watching the story of someone you think is getting ripped off is almost like an auto accident. Everybody wants to stop and take a look to see what's going to happen next.

The bottom line was that his style was different from any of the other infomercials on TV that night. I watched it for at least 7 or 8 minutes. I don't watch infomercials for any longer than 30 to 45 seconds, usually.

Here's my question for you. Can you find a unique, different, or totally opposite way to present the information that you have to offer? Can you find a way to appeal to the doubters and critics? How do you know? Have you tried? If you haven't tried, you'll never know until you do.

By taking a contrarian look at your content and approach, you might discover new opportunities for improvement.

Mistake 65: Relying on Just One Source of Traffic

"Don't put all your eggs in one basket."

There are literally hundreds of ways to drive traffic and sales on the Internet. While you'll never use most of them, you should use a good mix of strategies to market your business online. Relying on just one source of traffic and sales to drive your online marketing efforts puts your business in a very dangerous position.

Why?

Let's say you decide to focus on SEO and all your traffic comes from Google's organic search rankings (the main rankings that appear on the left side of the search results page).

What happens if Google changes their algorithm and instead of being ranked #1 for your top keyword, you're dropped to #483 overnight (yes, this does happen!)? What if your top competitors figure out how to leap ahead of you in the rankings and people visit their sites instead of yours?

What if Microsoft's Bing search engine delivers better search results and people flock to them instead of using Google?

There actually are online business models that rely on Google for virtually all their traffic. It's great when it works, but what happens when it doesn't?

If you rely on one company to drive your site's traffic and/or revenue, you're not in charge of your business. Outside forces beyond your control can conspire against you and put you out of business very quickly.

So the simple way to avoid this is to diversify your online marketing efforts. Get traffic to your website from multiple sources – organic search, paid search, social media, banner ads, affiliates, video marketing, article marketing, and more. The more sources of traffic you have, the less the impact of any one of those sources drying up will be. That gives you more control over your business and puts it in a much stronger position.

Mistake 66: Caring More About Your Sales Process than a Customer's Buying Process

Ever dealt with a sales rep who was such a schmuck that you almost didn't even want to buy what you came for anymore? All the rep had to do was take your order. You knew what you wanted, but unfortunately, the rep had just had been taught how to lead the customer through their sales process by a manager who was watching closely, and since the rep probably valued their job, they did what the boss expected them to do.

It would have been better if the company who was trying to sell you that product had been more sensitive to your buying process instead of getting wrapped up in their sales process.

An alternative solution to this problem is easy. Make the answers to your buyers' remaining questions available another way (like using online web videos, podcasts, blogs, etc.).

Mistake 67: Failing to Offer Your Products or Services for Sale Online Using eCommerce

What company doesn't want customers to buy from them as soon as possible, if not right away? They pretty much all do, right?

Then why do so many of them create a sales process that builds in unnecessary delays? If a prospect wants to buy before or after hours, are they supposed to wait? If the product isn't available online, then the answer is yes, but of course, that answer is not ideal.

Mistake 68: Letting Egos and Attitudes Kill Sales

Have you ever heard experts or sales trainers say that customers buy from people they like? If so, you have to wonder if the opposite is true as well.

If it is, then that means customers won't buy from people they don't like. Salespeople are human beings. Some have attitudes and others have big egos. Both can turn off prospects.

When companies use web videos, blogs, podcasts, review sites, and websites to answer prospects' questions and demonstrate value online without all the attitude or ego, bad things don't often happen and good things often do.

Mistake 69: Making Customers Jump Through Too Many Hoops

How do you feel when you have a problem with a product or service that you just bought and you have to spend what seems like an eternity giving your name and customer ID along with a detailed description of your problem to three different people before you can find someone that can help you solve it?

What if you need help at 7:09 p.m. and you call the store for customer service or technical support only to find out that they closed at 5:00 and won't be open until Monday morning? You're going to suffer.

Unless you want your current customers to become unhappy past customers, don't make the same mistake. If you truly know your customers and the problems that they face, create a virtual customer service platform consisting of autoresponders, videos, podcasts, blogs, and articles that give them the answers they need fast and easy on your website 24 hours a day, 7 days a week, 365 days a year.

Your customers could actually have the solutions to their problems in less time than it normally takes to get a live and knowledgeable person on the phone to explain it to them.

Mistake 70: Not Doing the Research

"Give me six hours to chop down a tree and I'll spend the first four sharpening the axe."
– Abe Lincoln

Here's a big secret about what separates the top copywriters from the herd. Yeah, they've got some writing chops. But that's NOT what makes them truly great. The thing that separates the truly great ones from the pack is their research skills.

Before they write a WORD of copy, they're immersing themselves in the product/service they're selling, the audience they're marketing to, and the competition.

- They ask the key questions of business owners, salesmen, inventors, etc., to find the golden nuggets that'll provide the foundation of the copy.
- They interview customers and prospects to understand what their needs are. (And not their superficial needs, their DEEP emotional needs that the product/service fulfills.)
- They keep digging until they've got the emotional hook that'll drive the copy that makes prospects *quiver* with desire, the bullet points that *tease and tantalize* their emotions, the offer that leaves prospects with little choice but to pull out their wallets and hand over their hard-earned cash.
- They'll uncover the company's Unique Selling Proposition that can be used to position them in a way that makes the competition largely irrelevant.

When it comes to marketing, research is your AXE. Ignore it at your own risk!

Mistake 71: Failure to Minimize Client Exposure to Human Error and Misunderstanding

Have you ever met customers who felt they were lied to by your sales or customer service staff? Or even if they weren't lied to and they just misunderstood what the sales or customer service rep said, there really hasn't been an easy way to prove what was said or what really occurred?

When customers are mad, they tell everyone they know. Some don't stop there, and they go online and tell people they don't know. Once those negative words are typed about your company online, they may never go away, and they can haunt you forever.

Any way you look at it, it's a bad situation, and it's one of the reasons I'm such a fan of using web videos, podcasts, blogs, review sites, and articles to answer prospects' questions. It's the ultimate quality control feature and eliminates any "he said, she said" arguments that nobody wins anyway.

Mistake 72: Paying Unnecessary Commissions

How much would your bottom line improve if your organization didn't have to pay salespeople commissions for their sales? What if you could get rid of some of their salaries, too, and maybe even increase your organization's sales?

You're probably thinking, "Yeah, that sounds great, but how do you do it?" Create a virtual sales force and customer service presence (blogs, podcasts, videos, articles, etc.). Once it's up there, it's not like you have to pay commissions or salary, but the darn thing keeps selling.

Mistake 73: Spending Time With Employee Drama Instead of Customers

How much easier would your life be if you didn't have to deal with the attitudes and counterproductive egos of your top salespeople? Good ones know they're good, and because they sell, many of them create all kinds of management headaches because they think their management team will put up with their nonsense.

Unfortunately, many managers DO put up with it. It doesn't have to be that way. Videos, blogs, podcasts, and articles that sell from your website don't talk back. They don't blow off sales reports. They don't complain. They don't set a bad example for up-and-coming salespeople, and they never have an off day.

Mistake 74: Monitoring Fiction Over Fact

Do you or your managers ever get tired of babysitting salespeople, or asking for sales reports that come in late or are full of fiction? Your decisions are only as sound as the facts on which they're based. If you don't know what kind of sales activity is really going on (or isn't going on), you're at a huge disadvantage.

Sales reps can tell you they went on sales calls when they were really hanging out at the local golf course or mall. They can tell you that they gave their presentations exactly like their sales manager taught them. But unless you want to play big brother or babysit grown adults, you can only hope they're telling the truth.

The best websites and video players will let you know what videos your prospects watched, how long they watched, where they exited, or what actions they took afterward. They can also reveal information that can give you additional insights into your ideal prospects that you would have never gotten from your staff.

Are they men? Are they women? Where are they from? What age group do they represent? Why guess when you don't have to?

Mistake 75: Losing Top Talent Unnecessarily

Do you realize how much it costs to recruit a single sales or customer service rep, much less a bunch of them? Costs of advertising available positions online, in local newspapers, and at career fairs, managing time scanning résumés, and doing interviews add up.

Since sales and customer service reps are often subjected to abusive and angry customers, those positions are notorious for high turnover. We're talking about expensive and ongoing recruiting.

For what? Face it. At some point, those jobs boil down to your company's ability to get the right answers to the same problems delivered to different customers and prospects.

For less than it typically costs to recruit a single customer sales or service rep, companies can produce a whole series of videos, blogs, podcasts, articles, and reviews that may even do a better job of impressing prospects and keeping customers happy.

Mistake 76: Paying Too Much for Sales Training

Are you sick of new sales reps blowing expensive leads? Regardless of their positive attitude and work ethic, sometimes their best just isn't good enough.

This happens all the time with new reps during their training period. Since sales jobs are high-turnover positions, that means there are usually a lot of new reps and blown leads.

The most expensive sales training there is takes place in front of qualified and interested prospects in the form of lost sales revenue from blown opportunities that should have been converted.

Promotional videos, blogs, podcasts, and articles don't make mistakes, and if their closing percentage isn't high enough based on the measurable number of prospects they reach and convert into customers, they can be changed.

Mistake 77: Lack of Knowledge When It's Needed Most

What happens when a new employee has a job to do, but the boss isn't around to tell them how to do something? Do they go for it and screw something up? Do they sit around and keep apologizing while the customer or coworker gets frustrated or leaves?

A good leader knows a job inside and out, and if they've done a job for any length of time before becoming the leader, then they know the answers to the questions they are frequently asked by new employees. Creating employee-training videos that can be watched on a computer, mobile phone, or wireless tablet gives employees access to the information they need to do their jobs, even if the leader isn't around.

If your goal is to have your employees do the right thing for your customers as soon as possible, then you might want to consider supplementing your existing employee training programs with video and podcast courses, too.

Mistake 78: Sending Employees Mixed Messages

What happens when different supervisors tell new employees different things? Answer? They screw stuff up, get embarrassed, and sometimes get fired or quit.

I had a friend once tell me that when it comes to training new employees, if you don't have a consistent standard, it's hard to measure the deviation. If you've got different leaders telling employees different things, then don't be surprised when they get frustrated and don't perform well.

As an alternative, I might suggest that you consider creating training videos that consistently teach your employees the best way to do their jobs without confusing them. As technology improves, it's never been more cost-effective for employees to be able to get the training they need and access it on their computers or even mobile devices.

Mistake 79: Allowing Institutional Knowledge to Escape

Screw the "old-timer."

So, your "old-timer" just walked out in a huff and quit. Good riddance! Right? Maybe not.

One of your biggest assets (institutional knowledge) just left and isn't coming back.

Unless you made a bunch of videos (that documented all the "right ways" to do things) before he left, you're SCREWED!

Mistake 80: Relying Too Heavily on Your Reps and Their Customer Relationships

It happens every day ... a trusted employee (or top sales rep) gets greedy. At some point they decide they are tired of making the boss look good and the owner rich and they decide to steal "THEIR" customers and start their own business.

Some make it. Others don't. But they all succeed in stealing some customers and creating unnecessary chaos.

Half the time, noncompete agreements don't do squat. Why risk it? Business videos that sell your stuff online (even while you sleep) don't steal your customers ... they create more of them.

Mistake 81: Assuming Your Ideal Prospects Like What YOU Like

Kirk Mooney is the general manager for a few radio stations on the outskirts of the St. Louis metropolitan area. In fact, one of his stations is located about 30 miles south of the city, just off a major interstate that lots of people drive every day on their morning commute to work.

I grew up in the area surrounding his station and couldn't believe it when he told me about the size and demographics of his listeners.

I grew up listening to KSHE-95, the St. Louis rock 'n' roll station that's been around since before I was born. Kirk smiled at me and said, "You may not like country music or ever listen to our station, but there are plenty of others who do."

There's a lesson here. My friend Karen Fox (see http://www.KarenTheConnector.com) tells her clients that "It's a big mistake to assume your target market is spending time on YOUR favorite social platform."

Mistake 82: Failing to Connect the Dots for Prospects and Customers

Steve Smart (see http://www.2QSolutions.net) is a BMW enthusiast and invests a lot of time on YouTube learning about BMW engines and how to work on them.

He told me about a video produced by a machine shop that he really liked. The name of the shop was included in the title, but further contact information or invitations to connect on social media platforms weren't offered.

Steve did some digging and eventually found the company's website. When he did, there was no reference to the great video on YouTube.com or any of the shop's other social media channels.

Don't make prospects or customers work too hard to find you. Steve shares this story with his customers and advises them to "connect the dots" for their prospects with branded social media platforms, websites, blogs, and other content sources that are congruent and seamlessly tied together.

Mistake 83: Inflexible/Inaccessible Content Management Systems and Websites

It happened again. This time it happened to one of my running buddies who also owns a construction company.

What happened? The guy who designed, hosted, and managed his website finally flaked out. At first, the web designer stopped returning calls. Then it took forever to get replies via email. There were things that needed to be changed on his site, but my friend (and his business) were being held hostage by a web designer who would not respond.

Cesar Keller (see http://www.SimpleFlame.com) has been designing websites for over 15 years and sees this happening all the time. It happens so often that one of the first things he tells his potential clients is to make sure they are able to control and manage their own content regardless of who they hire to help them build a website. Content these days can be managed with levels of simplicity that rival word processors.

Mistake 84: Forgetting There's No F***ing Erase Button on the Internet

Go to Google.

Type in "Chrysler F Bomb Tweet"

Yes, Chrysler representatives deleted that Tweet a few years ago.

Clearly, it did not go away. You can still read about it.

Lesson learned?

Mistake 85: Creating Sites/Content That Is Not Mobile-Friendly

Brandon Dempsey (see http://www.GoBrandGo.com) was recognized by the SBA as the Young Entrepreneur of the Year and mentioned in *Forbes*. He's a friend of mine, and I've always felt he had his finger on the pulse of what trends were emerging in business and why.

He was one of the first among my circle of friends that predicted by 2015, if not sooner, more people will visit websites using mobile devices than desktop computers.

If he's right, and I think he probably is, then you don't want to be creating sites or content that doesn't scale well on mobile devices.

Mistake 86: Failure to Recognize and Build Your Goldmine (Your Prospect and Customer Lists)

This is a biggie. You can have a tribe of followers on YouTube, Facebook, Twitter, Pinterest, LinkedIn, etc.

If you want to reach the subscribers on YouTube, then create a new video. If you want to reach those who "liked" your Facebook page, then create a post and promote it. Using social media platforms, you can communicate with people where they are and where they like hanging out. That's good.

Want to know what is GREAT? Get those people on YOUR email and/or contact lists and you'll find out. Your list of prospects and customers may end up being one of your most valuable assets and a source of many future leads and sales.

Russell Brunson (see http://www.DotComSecrets.com) once told me that a name on an email list that a prospect or customer opted into in

exchange for one of your special offers should be worth between $1 and $6 per month to your business. Of course, you need to communicate with them regularly, express your personality so they get to know you better, and provide additional value
on a regular basis. But assuming you do, these are the people you present with offers to buy your products or services.

The people on your list should like, trust, and value you. Because they do, they are also the ones who will buy from you if you ask them to.

I'm a fan of InstantCustomer.com, MarketVolt.com, AWeber.com, and MailChimp.com. There are plenty of good autoresponder and email list management options available to choose from. Pick one.

Mistake 87: Being Afraid to Invest in Paid Online Advertising

It's no secret that I am becoming less of a fan of traditional (radio, TV, newspaper, magazine, etc.) advertising for a wide range of reasons. However, paid online advertising, if done correctly, can generate revenue in excess of costs and get you and your products introduced to people in your market you might not otherwise have reached.

I was visiting with the publisher of a community newspaper one day and he told me that businesses pretty much "had to" advertise in his local publication because he had the largest audience in the county. He also informed me that businesses really needed the exposure to local residents in the area and that advertising in his paper was the best way to get that exposure in the close-knit community served by his print publication.

He was wrong on both counts. It would be a safe bet to say that Google and maybe even Facebook had a greater reach in his targeted local area.

If a business owner just wanted to get "awareness," they could buy pay-per-click ads that would show up whenever local folks were online and just offer some "special" that wouldn't be good enough to get anyone to click on it. Since area business owners would only have to pay a small fee every time someone clicked on their online advertisement, by writing a bad ad that nobody would click on, they would still get their name brand "exposure" without spending much, if anything.

Am I suggesting that businesses should create crummy ads designed to fail so they will get name recognition without having to pay? NO. I'm just saying that the two main selling points presented by the newspaper shouldn't have been considered selling points to an educated marketplace of business owners.

Is there a place for paid online advertising? Yes. If it generates more profit than it costs, do it.

Even "free" online marketing has a cost. There is a cost in terms of the time necessary to create and populate online and social media content outlets with your material. So it's not really "free" either.

Josh Turner is the founder of http://www.LinkedSelling.com and http://www.LinkedUniversity.com and specializes in helping clients use LinkedIn as a business development tool.

He knows who his best clients are, specifically. He knows what industries his ideal prospects work in. He knows what geographical locations they work in. He knows how old they are. He knows what kind of job titles they have. He knows what their interests are. He knows what they value.

He also does the work to create targeted ad copy featuring special offers his ideal clients would value greatly (usually access to free educational webinars that solve common problems faced by his prospects). Then he invests wisely to make sure his ads get placed in front of his ideal clients. As long as he generates more profit from sales made to those prospects than it costs him in advertising fees and the value of his time, it's a winning move. To assume that highly targeted online advertising is a waste of money is a mistake.

Mistake 88: Being Busy Instead of Productive

Don Harkey is a partner at the People Centric Consulting Group in Springfield, Missouri (see http://www.peopleccg.com), and he was telling me about how his team was working with a company focused on improving stagnant sales revenue. The company had been around a long time, was well known, offered products and services that were in demand, and did it at a fair price. Competition wasn't their main problem either.

Don interviewed their salespeople and told me of a conversation he had with one of them who was putting in more than enough hours of work each week, but was still falling far short of his achievable sales goals. Don asked him what tactics he was employing to generate leads.

The sales representative proceeded to showcase a long list of community networking groups and regional civic organizations he was involved in. He met lots of people and got tons of business cards. Don actually went with this sales rep to a few events and was pleasantly surprised to learn that practically everybody knew and liked this particular sales rep.

Then the frustrated underperforming sales rep told Don, "I don't even have time to follow up on all of my proposals." What? Really? Don had to ask, "You don't have time to close sales because you are too busy networking?"

The rep used tactics that generated leads. However, having an inefficient and unsystematized strategy for converting leads into orders resulted in poor follow-up. Lack of clear priorities didn't help either.

Allen Minster, coauthor of the book *Sales Utopia*, used to often say that "Time kills deals." I agree.

Bill Prenatt (see http://www.simplysuccessful-llc.com) was a St. Louis area sales executive who led a food sales team from $100 million in sales to nearly $250 million per year before he became a consultant. He always asked his struggling sales reps, "Are you busy or productive?"

Sometimes being busy instead of productive is the fault of the salesperson because they make poor choices in regard to their priorities and time management. Sometimes, there are poor (or no) automated lead generation and conversion strategies or systems in place. Or it can also be a combination of both.

Don ended up helping the company put together a clear marketing and sales strategy. He helped them identify their ideal prospects, appropriate and congruent messaging, and the best "modes" to deliver the message to the market. He also helped them develop systematized methods of consumer education and follow-up so prospects could become clients as efficiently as possible.

Here's the bottom line: Don also made sure salespeople invested and prioritized their time in ways that served live prospects and customers utilizing their specific knowledge and expertise. "Busy work" was identified and channeled through automation and systems where it could be processed more efficiently.

If you aren't examining "the old ways" of doing things because you or your staff members are too busy, it could be a mistake. It might be harder to spot or accept as a mistake if you're making a decent profit or hitting goals. However, if you consider the probability that the profit you are currently earning is only a FRACTION of what it could be COULD be, it's still a mistake.

Mistake 89: Focusing on Traffic, Not Conversions

Imagine you're about to open a big retail store. You hire a talented architect and design team and they knock it out of the park. I mean this thing is spectacular ... the window display, the interior ... you could not have asked for anything better.

And in your excitement to open your doors to the public, you kind of let a few things fall by the wayside. You don't train your sales staff. You carelessly scatter your inventory across the store. And you stick your cash registers in this out-of-the-way place so no one's really quite sure where to check out.

Do you think that store would struggle with sales? Of course it would!

And how would you fix that problem? Would you …

A. Try and drive as much foot traffic through the front door as possible, or
B. Train the sales staff, fix the inventory issues, and move the cash registers?

Clearly B would be the best choice.

But faced with a similar situation on your website, I bet most of you would go for the traffic.
I say that because most business owners come to me thinking they have a traffic problem. But in more cases than not the real problem with their website is not a lack of traffic—it's a lack of conversions.

A conversion can be a purchase someone makes on your website. Or it could be an action they take to get into your sales funnel: signing up for your newsletter, downloading a whitepaper, calling you.

Having a great looking site that gets lots of traffic is great … but if you take that to the bank and try to deposit it, the teller is, at best, gonna laugh at you, and if she's having a bad day, she may end up calling security!

Conversions are what bring in the cash!

You could be a traffic ninja and have thousands of people coming to your website ... tomorrow!

But if you don't have your conversion house in order, most of that traffic would be wasted.

Now, am I saying that just sending more traffic to your website is a bad idea? NO!! Sending more traffic to your site will probably produce more leads and sales for you.

But what I am saying is that if you're not focusing on conversions, your results could be so much better! And, if you're gonna spend the time and money and effort to drive that traffic to your website, then you should make the most of it!

Think of your website as this big ocean trawler net. And if you're not focused on conversions, your net has gaping holes in it and customers and revenues that should be yours ... that are within your grasp ... are slipping away.

Plug the holes in your net. Fix your conversion problem. And I promise you, if you do, you will fix your traffic problems.

Summary

In summary, you now know what trends are emerging and why. You know the importance of good keyword research. You know the importance of creating lots of useful and compelling content that serves your ideal prospects as well as other service providers who take care of the same ideal prospects you do. You understand the importance of creating your content in all different formats (blogs, articles, videos, podcasts, social media posts, etc.). You understand the power of video and YouTube marketing to sell your products, solve customer problems, and train employees online without having to add or manage unnecessary additional headcount. You also know the importance of putting your content and ideas in all the places where your ideal customers can be found. You know about the most common mistakes and how to avoid them.

We wrote this book so we could contribute to your success as others have contributed to ours. The rest is up to you. Don't waste what you now know. You're ready.

SECTION 3: The Bonuses (Did we save the best for last? You be the judge.)

Super Bonus Strategy #1: - DEFENDING YOUR GOOD NAME

Let's pretend that you own Johnny's Auto Repair in Anytown, Missouri. Let's also pretend that you advertise like crazy on radio and TV, in newspapers and magazines, and even online. You drive hundreds of people a week to your auto repair shop. Things couldn't be better, right?

Wrong. What if your repair shop was surrounded by people walking up and down the sidewalks all around your building carrying picket signs that say "Johnny's Auto Repair Sucks!" What if they were yelling "Johnny ripped us off" through bullhorns that were so loud you couldn't even think clearly? What if they did it 24 hours a day, 365 days a year, and you couldn't make them leave?

You would have a HUGE problem. MORE advertising wouldn't solve it, because even though it could get people to come TO your auto repair center, it probably couldn't get them to come IN because of all of those protesters walking the streets.

Well, this kind of thing happens online every day. It might even be happening to you right now. It could happen to you in the future. The worst part is that the "protesters" online (i.e., the people who write bad reviews and try to damage your reputation online) could be relatives or friends of your competitors who are intentionally trying to smear you. Or maybe your staff did make an honest mistake and tried to fix it, but the customer was just impossible to please no matter what you did.

In any case, if people type your company name, product name, or service name into search engines and the first page of results features "haters" calling you out (justified or not) and telling people to BEWARE of your company in big, bold ALL CAPS (which is how they often act when they're mad), then your prospects will notice it.

They will notice it when they go online to find your location, phone number, or hours of operation. They will notice it when they go to look for reviews of your company, products, or services. They will look you up on their mobile device while they're standing in front of your service desk, especially if the estimate is an expensive one.

As long as the "haters" have a place on the first page of search results for your company name and location, products, or services, you've got a BIG problem.

Since approximately 9 out of 10 people never look past page one on a search, if you put out content that bumps the "haters" to the second page of search results, you have MINIMIZED POTENTIAL DAMAGE by nearly 90%.

If your auto repair shop made $1,000 from each transmission you repaired, how many of those opportunities would you lose each month because the online "haters" scared away your best prospects? How many would you lose each year, and how many years would you lose those opportunities until you decided to do something about it?

That's just transmission jobs. Want to add up how much you would lose on brake jobs, radiator jobs, starter jobs, oil changes, electrical system repairs, and so on?

First of all, it's a GREAT idea to buy a URL with your name on it. It's also a GOOD idea to buy another one with your name and town included. At a minimum, it might not hurt to get some sites put up that have some basic information about what you offer, hours of service, and locations, and maybe add a blog that you update once a month with tips and helpful ideas.

If you don't want to add the expense of creating and maintaining more websites, hold on to your URLs because you might need them later, and go with a video strategy that is easier, faster, and more inexpensive (and often works just as well if not better if you do it right). To protect against "haters" in the future or to push down and bury the "haters" that are already there, put out YouTube videos that have been titled, tagged, scripted, and described properly. To find out how, see "Secret Weapon #3" in the "Want More Views?" menu option of http://www.BusinessWebVideos.com.

Super Bonus Strategy #2 - Using YOUR COMPETITORS' Advertising Budget Against Them (This one is a doozy!)

We've got some good news and some bad news. We'll start with the bad news first.

We are going to upset LOTS of apple carts with the ideas that we are about to share. Lots of people are going to hate us (i.e., your competitors and the companies who sell them advertising).

The good news is that YOU can be the beneficiary. You've purchased this book. You've read more than 99% of the population ever would, and we've saved the best for last, strategically speaking.

WARNING: This strategy will take guts. You might even get calls or letters from your competitors' lawyers. Talk to your own lawyer before you implement the ideas and strategies we're about to share if you have any concerns at all.

It's not for sissies, and if you just want to "get along" with your competitors and "be friends," then this isn't for you. If you want to outsmart, outmaneuver, and dominate (so they have to write a HUGE check to buy you out), then you're going to LOVE this. So here it goes.

Ask yourself this: What is one of the main purposes of investing in traditional advertising? What do the people trying to sell you advertising like to offer you as one of their main selling points? It's name recognition, right?

Isn't that one of the main reasons you're told to buy television, radio, and newspaper ads? You are told that when people recognize a need or a want for what you have to offer, you want them to remember your company name, right?

In the old days, if you advertised "successfully," your prospects would remember your name and go to the Yellow Pages to look up your phone number or get the address so they knew where you were located, right?

Now they get on a mobile phone, tablet, or computer and use search engines to get the information they want about you, your company, and your products or services.

What if I told you that it might not be such a great idea to try and outspend your biggest competition using traditional advertising? What if I told you that the more your competitors spent on traditional advertising, the BETTER it could be for you? That's right. You might actually WANT your competitors to spend their profits on advertising in efforts to get more people to remember their name. Want to know how to increase your PROFIT when your COMPETITORS increase THEIR traditional advertising budgets?

Let's pretend that you own a small independent company. Because you work from home and keep overhead low, you have the advantage of offering the same quality or better-quality products or services at a much lower price. The disadvantage you THINK you have is that all of your big-name competitors have HUGE radio, TV, and newspaper budgets and have earned really good name recognition in your market.

In this example, we'll call your biggest competitor BRAND X and assume they advertise like crazy and have great name recognition, and lots of your ideal prospects are typing THEIR names and products into search engines when they recognize a need.

Make no mistake, BRAND X will have a website, and it is likely to come up in search engine results, but what about all the OTHER listings on the same results page? What if they were YOURS? That is why the "jug fishing" approach to online marketing we talked about earlier is a MUST.

This is why it is SO important to make sure you create all kinds of content, in all kinds of different formats (videos, blogs, articles, podcasts, status site/social media posts, etc.), and put them out to as many places as possible.

What if there were multiple videos comparing advantages and disadvantages of BRAND X's product A, B, or C to YOUR company's product A, B, or C? What if there were alternative websites listed that YOU OWNED and managed and you called them something like BRANDXREVIEWS.COM? What about Facebook or other social media posts or podcasts TIED TO YOUR company accounts that mentioned BRAND X and contained discussions around product advantages and disadvantages and LINKS TO ALTERNATIVE products (i.e., yours)?

We have executed this strategy in several different niches, and here's what we learned.

In an effort to get traffic from people looking for Competitor A, Competitor B, and Competitor C who were all located in the same geographic region, we put together a video series promoting the top service providers in the region. In an effort to rank in search engines for THEIR names, we included the names of the top companies in the area along with our client's company name.

To the outside world, it came off like a promotional campaign for the industry and the region, and our client actually got a call from the owner of another company in the same region whose "feelings were hurt" because their lesser-known company's name wasn't mentioned in the series. The reason the lesser-known company wasn't included in the series is because we did the research ahead of time and found out that there weren't enough prospects looking for their company online to make it worthwhile to include them. Our client apologized for the "oversight" and we just smiled.

Yes, this is an aggressive strategy. It's like surrounding all your competitors by putting YOUR stores on every side of all their physical locations, except that you're doing it online. Before prospects can get to them, it will be hard for them not to notice

YOU. Once you "own" that virtual real estate all around your biggest competitors' best product, service, and location searches online, it's a huge asset for you. It will only make your company more desirable and likely to get acquired for more money.

We mentioned the possibilities of getting contacted by lawyers. It should go without saying, but we'll say it anyway: Do not be deceptive, misrepresent, or disparage. If you do, then don't be surprised if you get letters from lawyers demanding you stop.

When reviewing or comparing Product A to Product B, list the advantages and disadvantages of each. Let the reader decide what's best for them. If you create a website called BRANDXREVIEWS.COM and BRAND X is a big name with deep pockets, do not be surprised if you get a letter from their legal representatives bullying and demanding that you turn over the domain name to them and/or cease operation of the site.

We have seen these letters and emails. If you decide to use this strategy and create review sites that mention competitors by name, we suggest that you place a message on the page indicating that your site is in no way affiliated with or a representative of BRAND X, and it might even be a good idea to provide the link to the BRAND X website so you have a defense against anyone claiming you are trying to misrepresent, confuse, or deceive site visitors.

Last time we checked, there is still freedom of speech and freedom of the press in America, and good luck making a case that it is illegal to criticize, review, or discuss brands and products. It's hard to find companies that would have deeper pockets than Wal-Mart. If their lawyers can't shut down WalmartSucks.org after 13 years (and you know they want to), then you should be able to compare and contrast your products and services with those of your competitors, especially if you do it in a professional, ethical, and accurate way.

Super Bonus Strategy #3 - Unleashing Our Top Four Secret Weapons
(For Video and Online Marketing)

Secret Weapon #1 - Want to know where to send your content and AUTOMATE your content distribution?

As of the date of this printing (subject to change), here are some great places to distribute your content in various formats. You may do it manually or use the link below to find out how to AUTOMATE the distribution of your content to most of the sites that are listed.

VIDEO SITES:

youtube.com

dailymotion.com

videobash.com

dekhona.com

iviewtube.com

metacafe.com

photobucket.com

tagworld.com

veoh.com

vidipedia.org

PODCAST SITES:

everypodcast.com

podcast.com

podcastblaster.com

plazoo.com

BLOG SITES:

blogger.com

tumblr.com

livejournal.com

squidoo.com

wordpress.com

SOCIAL BOOKMARKING SITES:

reddit.com

slashdot.org

bibsonomy.org

folkd.com

memotoo.com

saveyourlinks.com

startaid.com

stumbleupon.com

whitelinks.com

STATUS SITES:

linkedin.com

pinterest.com

facebook.com

twitter.com

plurk.com

sokule.com

friendfeed.com

ARTICLE SITES:

ezinearticles.com

articlecity.com

articletrader.com

articlecube.com

articlesnatch.com

earticlesonline.com

homebiztools.com

blogwidow.com

premierdirectory.org

searcharticles.net

triond.com

workoninternet.com

look-4it.com

Doing it manually takes a long time. This is a MUCH better way.

Here's our affiliate link. They pay us a referral fee (without raising the cost to you), but we would recommend this service even if they didn't.

Link to our favorite automated content distribution system:

http://www.TrafficGeyser.com/cmd.php?af=75353

Take advantage of the trial period while it is available. It's not expensive and lasts a few weeks. We use it. We recommend it and think it is well worth it.

Secret Weapon #2 - Want to introduce your YouTube channel and videos to HUNDREDS of TARGETED and ACTIVE users EACH DAY who are MUCH more likely to SPREAD THE WORD about you and your expertise?

It is almost like getting introduced to tons of folks every day in a warm market. It's AUTOMATED (so it doesn't take much time) and saves you from the rejection that cold callers and telemarketers deal with all the time.

Here's the affiliate link (yes, they pay us a referral fee):

https://www.tubeassist.com/?a=TA222

Secret Weapon #3 - Our favorite keyword research tool: Get found on search engines.

If you would like your videos to be found on search engines, it is imperative to use keywords. We have used these strategies successfully for many businesses over the years.

1. Be sure to include your target Keyword Phrase or Phrases in the Title of your video.

2. Remember to include your target Keyword Phrase or Phrases in the Description of your video.

3. Don't forget to include your target Keyword Phrase or Phrases in the Script/Content of the video, and make sure you speak clearly.

4. It's important to include your target Keyword Phrase or Phrases in the TAGS when you upload your video as well.

CAUTION! If you don't know the best keywords, your online marketing and targeted traffic will suffer.

Link to our favorite keyword research tool:

http://www.marketsamurai.com/c/buildatribe

(Yes, it is an affiliate link, and we will earn a few bucks if you buy it. Yes, we would recommend it even if we didn't. Yes, we use it, too.)

Secret Weapon #4 - Get Professional Videos Produced for 90-95% Less Than Other High-End (High-Definition) Studios

Don't want to buy all the equipment to produce videos?

Never satisfied with how you look or sound on camera?

Don't have the time to shoot and produce videos yourself?

Want to invest 90-95% less than other high-end HD video studios charge to have someone else produce your videos for you?

Link to our "Done For You" Video Production Services:
http://www.BusinessWebVideos.com

Super Bonus GIVEAWAY #4 - We have a BIG SURPRISE for YOU!

If the video is still up, there's a REWARD available for you and you owe it to yourself to claim it before it goes away.

This may be available for a limited time only, so hurry over to http://www.AttractCaptureConvertBook.com and get yours while you still can!

Attract, Capture & Convert

About the Authors:

Mason Duchatschek

Mason Duchatschek is an online marketing strategist and entrepreneur who helps business owners attract, capture, and convert more of their ideal prospects into customers both online and offline, even if they find web and social media marketing options overwhelming.

As a true "multi-preneur," Mason heads the companies AMO-Employer Services, Inc. (see http://www.ReverseRiskConsulting.com) and Buildatribe, LLC, (see http://www.Buildatribe.com and http://www.BusinessWebVideos.com), which have helped over 1,000 companies maximize the capabilities of social media and web marketing technologies and the people who implement them. He has provided consulting, speaking, and thought leadership to major corporations such as Miller Brewing, Land O'Lakes, and Purina Mills.

Over the last 20 years, he has coauthored the books *Sales Utopia: How to Get the Right People, Doing the Right Things, Enough Times* with Allen Minster and *Attract, Capture & Convert: 89 Simple Ways Entrepreneurs Make Money Online (& Offline) Using Social Media & Web Marketing Strategy* with Adam Burns and Adam Kreitman.

His ideas have been featured in *Selling Power, Entrepreneur Magazine, The New York Times*, and Fox News.

Adam Burns

Adam Burns started out working part-time at minimum wage for a local sporting goods store 20 years ago and worked his way up to the position of chief operating officer of an eight-location family-owned regional sporting goods chain operating in three states with over 300 employees. Burns has invested countless 14- to 18-hour days working alongside his mentor Mason Duchatschek, exploring and testing strategies related to Facebook marketing, Pinterest marketing, YouTube marketing, Twitter marketing, blog marketing, podcasting, article marketing, and more. Burns was asked by Mason to contribute his perspective and experiences to this book.

Adam Kreitman

Adam Kreitman is an online marketing strategist who got his start in Internet marketing because of drug testing … but it's probably not in the way you think.

You see, he was president of a small, struggling drug testing company that needed clients. But the idea of making cold calls, knocking on doors, or spending a small fortune on Yellow Pages and print ads was a vile one. So he had to come up with another way to get qualified, motivated prospects in the door.

And it didn't take long before he discovered one: Google AdWords – a fairly new (at that time) online advertising program.

AdWords proved to be more than just a great way to drive highly qualified leads to the drug testing company's website. It was the best market research tool he'd ever come across as well (and having worked in market research, he's seen them all).

Using AdWords, Adam discovered a whole new market for the drug testing company that was bigger than the ones the company had traditionally been in.

At that point the lightbulbs over his head didn't just go off – they started exploding. And ever since then he's been hooked (on online marketing, not drugs)!

He quickly realized that it was a heck of a lot more fun to help business owners leverage the Internet to grow their businesses than it was to chase drug users around. So he left the world of drug testing and founded <u>Words That Click</u>, a firm specializing in PPC and conversion optimization, in 2007.

Adam is also a regular contributor to the highly respected conversion and design blog The Daily Egg. He was the Internet marketing expert for the show *The Rise to the Top* on ABC-TV. And he's also been named to a list of "Smokin' Hot Pieces of Brain Candy" along with Seth Godin, Alan Weiss, and Jeffrey Gitomer (seriously, Google it!).

For additional info, see

http://www.Buildatribe.com
http://www.BusinessWebVideos.com
http://www.WordsThatClick.com

Social Media:

Twitter:
http://www.Twitter.com/BuildTribes
http://www.Twitter.com/WordsThatClick

YouTube:
http://www.YouTube.com/Buildatribe
http://www.YouTube.com/BusinessWebVideos

Facebook:
http://www.Facebook.com/Buildatribe

Pinterest:
http://www.Pinterest.com/Buildatribe

Made in the USA
San Bernardino, CA
21 November 2014